THE LONDON SCHOOL OF LINGUISTICS:

A Study of the Linguistic Theories
of B. Malinowski and J. R. Firth

THE LONDON SCHOOL OF LINGUISTICS:

A Study of the Linguistic Theories of B. Malinowski and J. R. Firth

D. TERENCE LANGENDOEN

RESEARCH MONOGRAPH NO. 46
THE M.I.T. PRESS, CAMBRIDGE, MASSACHUSETTS

P
81
.G7
.L3

To my wife
Sally

Foreword

This is the forty-sixth volume in the M.I.T. Research Monograph Series published by The M.I.T. Press. The objective of this series is to contribute to the professional literature a number of significant pieces of research, larger in scope than journal articles but normally less ambitious than finished books. We believe that such studies deserve a wider circulation than can be accomplished by informal channels, and we hope that this form of publication will make them readily accessible to research organizations, libraries, and independent workers.

HOWARD W. JOHNSON

Preface

This work is a revision of my doctoral dissertation "Modern British Linguistics: A Study of Its Theoretical and Substantive Contributions" completed in 1964 under the supervision of Professor Noam Chomsky. Except for the addition of an appendix to Chapter 3 dealing with John Lyons' *Structural Semantics: An Analysis of Part of the Vocabulary of Plato*, and the elimination of a chapter dealing with the work of Sir Alan H. Gardiner, only relatively minor changes in the thesis have been made.

I especially wish to thank Professor Chomsky, whose influence on the writer is apparent throughout this work, and also Professor Henry A. Gleason, Jr., of the Hartford Seminary Foundation, for his constant encouragement throughout the writing of the thesis itself.

Columbus, Ohio   D. TERENCE LANGENDOEN
January 1967

Contents

THE LONDON SCHOOL OF LINGUISTICS:

A Study of the Linguistic Theories
of B. Malinowski and J. R. Firth

Introduction

This book is intended to acquaint linguists and others interested in the development of linguistics in this century with the character of the dominant school of descriptive linguistics in Great Britain today. That school can quite fairly be called the creation of one man, John Rupert Firth, and its date of origin can be given as 1944, the year in which Firth acceded to the Chair of General Linguistics at the University of London. He held this position until his retirement in 1956, and his death in 1960 (in the words of R. H. Robins) marked "the end of an era in the study of linguistics in Great Britain" (1961, p. 191). Because of Firth's long association with the University of London, the school has come to be known as the "London school," and we shall follow that usage. Like other geographic labels for schools in linguistics, this particular one is not entirely felicitous, inasmuch as the linguistic school of Daniel Jones, which we do not consider in this work, is equally deserving of this designation. Furthermore, London was and continues to be only one of the locations of this school, outposts of which are now located in many other academic centers throughout the United Kingdom, and indeed the Commonwealth.

Firth's entry into the field of linguistics in the early 1930's was certainly not a conspicuous one — details are given in Robins' obituary article just quoted from — and most important for an understanding of his later work is the fact that he participated in the seminars conducted at that time by the anthropologist Bronislaw Malinowski at the University of London.

1

Indeed, to understand most of the important aspects of Firth's work, it is necessary to be acquainted with Malinowski's linguistic studies. These studies have up to the present time been almost completely ignored by both anthropologists and linguists, and this is particularly unfortunate since Malinowski was one of the few important anthropologists of his time, and the only one in Great Britain, to have had an abiding interest in language itself. A critical analysis of this work, if only to supply a background for the later work of Firth, has therefore long been needed.

Such a critical analysis, when accomplished, turns out to have other values as well. First it sheds light on the steady change in theoretical orientation that Malinowski underwent from his earliest writings in the 1910's down to his latest publications in the early 1940's. It makes sense, in fact, to draw a line somewhere in the early 1920's, and to speak of work done before that time as representative of the "early" Malinowski and of work done after that time as being that of the "later" Malinowski. This cleavage is appropriate not only to his linguistic work but to his anthropological work as well. *Argonauts of the Western Pacific* stands to *Coral Gardens and Their Magic* much as Wittgenstein's *Tractatus* stands to his *Philosophical Investigations*, though not for the same reasons.

Roughly speaking, the early Malinowski maintained a rich theoretical position that far exceeded those of his contemporaries in terms of the number and kinds of assumptions he was willing to make concerning the structure of society and the relationship of the individual to it. Compared to his empirically oriented contemporaries, Malinowski seems almost a rationalist, one who believed not only in the reality of institutions and relationships, like Durkheim, but in their psychological reality. He also expressed belief in the existence of universal abstract entities in anthropological theory, whose actual manifestation could take different forms in different societies but which were generally expressible as rules for social conduct. While individual natives are generally unable to formulate them explicitly, they are usually able to determine their consequences in particular situations.

The later Malinowski, by contrast, espoused a much weaker theoretical position, one based on the tenets of behavioristic psychology. This is most clearly seen in his *Coral Gardens*, published in 1935 after the seminars in which he and Firth participated, and it is reasonable to suppose that Firth, always effective in arguing his position, actually had a considerable influence on Malinowski during the time that they worked together. This suggests that Firth had a well-defined theoretical framework of his own and that in formulating his linguistic position he simply fitted key concepts from Malinowski into this framework, while at the same time encouraging Malinowski's drift toward a radical form of behaviorism. There is reason to believe that Malinowski resisted this drift to some extent; even in *Coral Gardens* certain passages have a definitely early Malinowski ring. But as far as his view of language was concerned, the drift was quite complete. Chapter 1 of this book is therefore devoted to a critical study of Malinowski's linguistic work, and forms a self-contained unit.

The second and third chapters are devoted to a study of the major linguistic writings of Firth; Chapter 2 deals with his work up to 1944, and Chapter 3 with his subsequent publications. A systematic study of and, one might say, commentary on the linguistic theories and notions propounded by Firth have also long been needed. The reasons for this are not hard to find. First, all of Firth's published writings on linguistic theory and, for that matter, all of his descriptive work are notoriously obscure and programmatic. This state of affairs has been readily admitted by his followers. Robins, for example, described Firth's publications as "all readable and stimulating, but programmatic rather than definitive, often allusive rather than explicit, and sometimes infuriatingly obscure on points obviously vital to the theory he was expounding" (1961, p. 198). Second, no one else has ever successfully presented an explicit formulation of the theories of the London school and showed the historical and theoretical connections between them and those of the American and continental linguists. Third, the total history of the development of the London school has never been attempted before, except in outline.[1]

Firth's attention, at least in his published writings, was restricted to considerations of phonology and semantics, and in each area he formulated a very distinct-sounding position. In semantics, he extended the later Malinowski's contextual theory of meaning to cover a wider range of cases than Malinowski's, and in so doing he also made certain modifications of it. Our contention in this book is that while Firth's ideas are of some interest for the general theory of style, they are of no interest at all for the study of meaning. The single most important reason for this is that Firth's view is based on the opinion that language is not "creative" and that a person is totally constrained essentially to say what he does by the given social situation. Firth recognized the possibility that a person might not say what was expected of him in a

---

[1] The best recent treatment is by Robins (1963). Firth's own discussion of his debt to Malinowski may be found in Firth (1957*b*).

given situation, but then all that can be said of such utterances is that they are inappropriate.[2] After Firth's death in 1960, however, J. Lyons completed under the direction of W. S. Allen and R. H. Robins a dissertation on semantics that not only made use of Firthian notions of semantics but also drew on the generative linguistic theory of N. Chomsky. The dissertation in its published form in 1963 doubtless represents the most important original contribution to semantic theory to come out of British linguistics since Ogden and Richards, and for this reason critical discussion of this work has been included as an appendix to Chapter 3.

In phonology Firth owed no debt to Malinowski, who never much concerned himself with the subject. Firth saw himself as a phonologist standing at the culmination of a long line of British phoneticians and orthoepists, starting in the Elizabethan period, his immediate forebear in this line being Henry Sweet. Three of his papers in linguistics are devoted to the historical study of selected phoneticians and orthoepists. British workers are treated by Firth in (1946, pp. 92–120 in 1957c), Americans in (1949, pp. 156–172 in 1957c), and Europeans who worked in India and Burma in (1936, pp. 54–75 in 1957c). Firth was strongly motivated by the desire to dispel the myth that linguistics began with the nineteenth-century comparativists (cf. Firth [1949, p. 139 in 1957c]: "it is all to the good that we should look back on a couple of thousand years without fear of being turned into pillars of salt. The German comparativists had so harnessed and blinkered Western European linguistics in the nineteenth century that nothing earlier could have much interest for linguistic science"). Firth clearly took an antiquarian's delight in uncovering the insights of sixteenth- to eighteenth-century phoneticians and spelling reformers, but though these papers are of some historical interest they will not be considered in detail here.

Despite his admiration for Sweet, Firth did not inherit any particular theory from him. The only reference in which Firth clearly indicates that he is "carrying on" from Sweet is in (1948b, p. 146 in 1957c), where he asserts, first, that the idea of consonant and vowel cardinalization was originally hit upon by Sweet, and second that he has finally made a concrete proposal for consonantal cardinalization parallel to Daniel Jones's well-known vowel cardinalization. Furthermore, it is not true that Firth consistently maintained one single phonological theory throughout his

---

[2] A parallel to this position can be detected in the Parmenidean position, expounded by Cratylus in Plato's dialogue of that name: one cannot say what is not true, or that what is false is unintelligible. Firth held roughly that what is inappropriate is unintelligible.

linguistic career. Actually, three stages in Firth's thinking on phonology can be distinguished. In his earliest papers in the early 1930's he propounded essentially orthodox Daniel Jones phonemics. By 1935, however, he had come to a position roughly equivalent to that of W. F. Twaddell in the latter's *On Defining the Phoneme*. Finally in 1948 he published an account of his theory of prosodic analysis, which in essence is very much like Z. S. Harris' theory of long components first expressed in 1945. Arguments to substantiate the validity of these assertions are given in Chapters 2 and 3.

It is not hard to determine the reasons for Firth's shift in thinking about phonology. He disavowed Jonesian phonemics because he came to believe at some time in the early 1930's that there was something wrong with the principle of complementary distribution for phonology (although it remained quite valid for purposes of orthography design). His rejection of the principle, unlike Halle's and Chomsky's rejection of it, was not for any logical reason but for an aesthetic one. He simply believed the principle to be *inappropriate*. If two classes of sounds are in complementary distribution, then the particular sounds appearing in one context are diagnostic of that context, and similarly for the sounds in the other contexts. If one then invokes the principle and merges the various sounds into phonemes, there is no phonological reflection of the diagnostic or signaling value of the particular sounds.

The theory of prosodic analysis was arrived at simply by pushing the decision to reject complementary distribution to its ultimate conclusion and still remain within the framework of a taxonomic phonological theory. Prosodic analysis is really nothing more than a notation for carefully distinguishing features in an utterance which are diagnostic of a particular environment from those which are not, and is thus in a curious way the reverse of a phonemic analysis in which (within certain limits) phonetic features uniquely characteristic of a particular environment are disregarded (that is, considered subphonemic).

Since 1948 a large number of British linguists have enthusiastically adopted Firth's prosodic analysis approach, and a considerable number of descriptions, covering a large number of languages, have been written by these linguists. Many of the articles in which these descriptions appear were written largely to justify the Firthian approach, notably those found in *Studies in Linguistic Analysis*, which appeared in 1957.[3] We have included a dozen of these articles for examination in Chapter 4; they were chosen either because of their intrinsic impor-

---

[3] See also the author's review of this book in Langendoen (1964).

tance as illustrations of particular features of prosodic analysis or because in them the taxonomic constraints imposed by the theory were either consciously or unconsciously broken. We note that in all of the cases in which the authors went beyond these constraints they did so to achieve some kind of descriptive adequacy. These latter articles must be considered to rank among the outstanding descriptive phonological publications in the linguistics literature of that period. In our discussion of these articles some attempt is made to restate the various phonological descriptions in terms of the generative phonological theory of Morris Halle and Noam Chomsky. These restatements are meant to be taken only as suggestive. They introduce nothing new by way of data in the languages under consideration and so should not be interpreted to reflect the statements of generative phonologists working independently on these languages.

With the exception of the second of John Bendor-Samuel's papers on Terena phonology and John Lyons' book on semantic theory, nothing published after 1960, the year of Firth's death, has been discussed critically in this book. Since that time, largely under the leadership of Michael A. K. Halliday, of the University of Edinburgh, and his student Robert M. W. Dixon, now of the University of London, a distinct new school of "neo-Firthian" linguistics has developed. No attempt to analyze the theoretical and substantive contributions of this school has been attempted in this book. For some critical discussion, the reader is referred to a number of recent articles and books by Paul M. Postal, Peter H. Matthews, and myself.[4]

[4] Postal (1964, pp. 97–117), Postal (1966), Matthews (1966), Langendoen (forthcoming *a*, *b*).

1. The Linguistic Views of B. Malinowski

1.1 "Classificatory Particles" (1920)

Malinowski's only published linguistic description was his paper "Classificatory Particles in the Language of Kiriwina," which appeared in 1920, two years after the completion of his ethnographic field work in the Trobriand Islands. In the paper, he expressed the hope that he would someday be able to write a grammar of Kiriwinian (1920, p. 67), but the hope was never fulfilled. The bulk of the description in the paper concerns itself with the grammatical character of a class of particles that are attached to numerals, adjectives, and demonstratives when they occur with nouns, or in certain cases when these words stand alone.

Throughout the paper, Malinowski asserted that there is a need for the development of a theory of semantics that will enable researchers in linguistics to probe more deeply into language structure; one that will serve also as a basis for explaining particular grammatical facts about language, both universal and particular. He argued that such a semantic theory would have to be connected closely with ethnographic theory, since an understanding of what people mean by what they say depends in part upon what their culture is. His view of the connection between language and culture seems to have been in accord with nineteenth-century thinking. He said that he was familiar, for example,

7

with the work of Humboldt on the Kawi language of Java, and his only criticism of Humboldt's work was that since he did not do personal field work on the language and culture, but based his study solely on secondary sources, he probably did not fully grasp the relationship between the Kawi language and culture (p. 36).

One of the reasons for the need of a semantic theory of language, Malinowski argued, is simply that without it a satisfactory grammatical analysis of a language is not possible. Formal criteria are not enough to provide a basis for grammatical analysis or even for classifying words into parts of speech. A case in point, he believed, was the problem of classifying Kiriwinian words into parts of speech:

> . . . in dealing with the grammatical character of the various formatives, we had to keep their meaning constantly before us. In trying to prove that an expression should be classed as a noun or adverb or adjective or a 'nominal demonstrative', we use semantic and not formal definitions. (p. 78)

The actual problem is of some interest. The solution showed to Malinowski's satisfaction that simple formal analysis fails to provide an adequate grammatical description of the language. He pointed out that there is, at first glance, a subclass of adjectives that, unlike other adjectives, fails to take any classifying particles. But, he asked, how does one know on purely formal grounds that this class is in fact a subclass of adjectives? If we establish as a formal criterion of membership in the adjectival class that a word takes a classifying particle when it occurs with a noun, and that otherwise it is a member of some other class (say adverbial), and thus obtain a neat formal cleavage between modifier words which occur with classifiers and those which do not, then the grammatically correct analysis is ruled out.

Malinowski meant by a "formal definition" of a grammatical category a definition of it in terms of diagnostic linguistic environments in which members of the category are allowed to occur. His objection to using such formally defined categories was simply that one cannot distinguish arbitrary definitions from those which possess some sort of deeper significance, that is, those which "correspond to real distinctions in human thinking and human Weltanschauung" (p. 66). He pointed out, further, that having recognized these particular words which do not occur with classifiers as a subclass of adjectives one can recognize them again in more complicated expressions (where other formally based definitions would not enable one to do so) without modifying the formal definition in some way (p. 67). Malinowski gave, then, a twofold justification for the particular solution to the grammatical problem posed. First, his solution preserved the possibility of providing a definition of the categories (adjective, adverb, noun, and so on) that corresponds to distinctions in human thinking and outlook, and second, it left one free to analyze correctly the constituents of complicated constructions without forcing one to redefine the categories formally.

The first task that Malinowski proposed for a semantic theory was that it must provide a basis for the definition of grammatical categories, particularly the universal ones. Malinowski's understanding of universal grammar was, roughly speaking, traditional school grammar; consequently he saw the need for a universal semantic definition of the traditional parts of speech, their "modifications" like cases and tenses, and certain grammatical relations like subject and predicate. He expressed agreement with Sir Alan Gardiner's contention that the notions subject and predicate were not at all understood in contemporary philology (p. 36). For the purposes of the paper, he accepted "simple semantic criteria in using the terms 'noun' and 'nominal' to denote words which stand for an individually considered and defined thing, the term 'adjective' for words denoting attributes ascribed to a thing, and so on" (p. 74). He felt that he had not gone nearly far enough; he criticized himself for making "an amateurish, extemporized use of grammatical terms" (p. 78), but he felt that he had successfully avoided the pitfall of simply borrowing wholescale the "rigid grammatical concepts . . . of Indo-European linguistics . . . which lead to wrong distinctions, to tearing asunder of natural grouping, to false perspective" (p. 78).

It should be remarked, however, that in his actual classification of Kiriwinian words into parts of speech, he went beyond the restraints set by his semantic definitions of them. In effect, once he had found certain formal characteristics of the classes of words fitting the semantic classification, he included in the same class words that failed to meet the semantic characterization but which possessed similar formal characteristics. Thus, for example, he classed as nouns certain words that had abstract significance in the language because of their formal similarity to words whose significance fitted the universal semantic definition for "noun."

Malinowski believed very strongly that once someone developed a semantic theory adequate to the tasks he set for it, it would play a significant role in guiding linguists in their investigations of the structure of languages. He expressed the heuristic value of such a theory in the following terms:

It must be remembered first that a scientific theory gives us, besides a body of rules, also definite mental habits. . . . Thus it was necessary first clearly to state the range of the classificatory particles, their main function and meaning. As soon as such a striking phenomenon was observed in the numerals, the theoretical interest and the impulse toward completeness would make their discovery inevitable in the demonstratives and adjectives as well. Again, the constructive desire for completeness imposes the principle to search for all the classifiers and to present them in an exhaustive list. Once tabulated, the differences in their nature — their meaning, their grammatical function, and their degree of obsoleteness — became patent. . . . Further research is thus stimulated, and this leads to the discovery of new facts. And so on; theoretical analysis compels us to see gaps in the facts and to formulate problems — this elucidates new facts, which must be submitted to theoretical analysis again, and so on, until the limit is reached, where further details would be too vague and too insignificant for observation. (p. 73)

It is worth pointing out that Malinowski saw the value of a theory about language only for the analyst coming in from the outside; it did not occur to him that a theory of the sort he envisioned might have value also in explaining the phenomenon of language acquisition by native children. This is not to say that Malinowski never considered the problem of language acquisition by children; in subsequent publications, in fact, he devoted considerable attention to this question.

In addition to providing the basis for the definitions of the categories and relations of universal grammar, Malinowski posed as another goal for semantic theory the ability to account for the particular grammatical facts of particular languages in terms of the semantic circumstances provided by the cultural environment in which the language is spoken — and for which it may be said to be adapted. Thus:

But the analysis of meaning again led us often to ethnographic descriptions. When defining the meaning and function of several of the formatives, we had to make excursions into ethnography, describe customs, and state social conditions. (p. 78)

These "excursions into ethnography" occur at half a dozen or so different points in the description, each one occurring in connection with a discussion of particular classificatory particles. Each one, typically, is meant to explain why particular particles exist and have the character that they do in the language. Thus, in describing the particles used when counting and modifying nouns designating bunches of fruit, especially betel-nut clusters, he stated:

There is no doubt that bunches of fruit must be an important class of objects to a tribe, where gardening is one of the main economic pursuits, and one in which the natives take an extreme interest and pride. But, speaking more specially of the expression for betel-nut bunches, fruit clusters are also important from another point of view. Gifts and payments and tributes are a very prominent feature of the social organization and public life in Kiriwina. . . . In these undivided bunches of betel-nut play a specially prominent part. . . . (p. 49)

Malinowski's argument is simply that the cultural importance of bunches of fruit in Kiriwina accounts for the existence of a special classificatory particle for each of several nouns designating bunches of fruit in the language. Similarly, there is a classificatory particle used only with a noun designating batches of fish, since batches of fish play an important role in the economic life of the island. After giving a brief description of a particular ceremony involving the exchanges of bunches of fish for yams, Malinowski argued:

This somewhat lengthy description of the *wasi* (fish and yam exchange) has been given to show how narrow and definite is the application of the formative *O YLO* — and also to show how necessary it is to give some ethnographic information if grammatical relations are to be fully understood. (p. 52)

These citations show the typical "explanation after the fact" character of Malinowski's use of these pieces of ethnographic information. An even more striking example is his discussion of the classification of the noun meaning "basket of yams." This noun, apparently, is the only one in the entire language that appears without any classificatory particle when modified by a numeral, demonstrative, or adjective. When and only when one counts baskets of yams does one use bare numeral stems in the Kiriwinian language. To account for this seemingly bizarre fact, Malinowski appealed to the social significance of baskets of yams in Kiriwina:

It must be realized, however, that the counting of baskets of yams in Kiriwina is counting *par excellence* . . . the counting of baskets of yams is undoubtedly the most important occasion on which numbers have to be recorded in Kiriwina. (pp. 53–54)

All of Malinowski's "explanations" of grammatical fact on the basis of cultural fact are similarly anecdotal in nature. On the basis of his attempts to provide such explanations, therefore, no theoretical assertions can be made to suggest that cultural facts in general explain the existence and nature of particular grammatical rules. His examples are, however, sufficiently suggestive to indicate that it may not be totally impossible to arrive eventually at such theoretical assertions.

Malinowski's views about the relationships between the semantic and grammatical description of a language and the description of the culture in which it is spoken are significantly different here from the views which he later came to express. In this paper, Malinowski contended that the grammatical and semantic description of a language forms an autonomous entity within a broader framework — the complete ethnographic description of a culture. The strictly ethnographic part of the description supplies a partial explanation for certain grammatical and semantic features of the language. Universal grammar contains universal grammatical categories and relations defined in terms of universal semantic categories. The universal semantic categories are themselves elements of a universal ethnographic theory, which is constructed out of considerations pertaining to man's nature and the nature of his environment.

1.2 *Argonauts of the Western Pacific* (1922)

In 1921, one year after the publication of "Classificatory Particles," Malinowski completed his first major ethnographic treatise concerning the Trobriand Islands, *Argonauts of the Western Pacific*, which was published the following year. In it Malinowski had little to say directly concerning linguistic theory or description, but he presented a fairly detailed sketch of ethnographic theory in which semantic theory had a part. There are certain features of this sketch that indicate, by their sharp contrast with the position that he was to hold later, the degree to which his theoretical perspective changed over the years.

In his introductory chapter to this book, Malinowski framed his ethnographic theory in terms of three major principles of ethnographic methodology. The principles correspond to the three aspects of social life that Malinowski believed the ethnographer must fit together into a unified description of a given society. The ethnographer must (1) provide an account of the organization of the society, an anatomy of its culture. This amounts to a codification of the superficially non-observable aspects of the social environment in which each member of the society finds himself. The ethnographer must fill in this framework with (2) a characterization of the "imponderabilia of actual life," or the "typical behaviour" of the people of the society (1922, p. 20). This amounts to a description of the directly observable aspects of the social environment, including how the people actually behave, how they express their feelings, motives, and so on. Then (3) he must collect characteristic narratives from the society, and especially typical comments that the people make concerning their own social structure. These narratives Malinowski called the "documents of native mentality," and they provide the evidence for knowing what is in the minds of the natives concerning their own society. Malinowski summarized these three aspects of social life as follows:

. . . in every act of tribal life, there is, first, the routine prescribed by custom and tradition, then there is the manner in which it is carried out, and lastly there is the commentary to it, contained in the natives' mind. (p. 22)

Malinowski stressed that the structure of a society cannot be observed directly either by the ethnographer or the native but that to the native it is a psychological reality. As late as 1926, he wrote:

The honourable citizen is bound to carry out his duties, though his submission is not due to any instinct or intuitive impulse or mysterious 'group-sentiment', but to the detailed and elaborate working of a system, in which every act has its own place and must be performed without fail. Though no native, however intelligent, can formulate this state of affairs in a general abstract manner, or present it as a sociological theory, yet every one is well aware of its existence and in each concrete case he can foresee the consequences. (1926, p. 42)

In this same work, Malinowski suggested several universals of social structure, and at the same time stressed their very abstract nature. One of these principles he called "symmetry of structure," which may manifest itself in a number of ways in particular cultures, for example in the way in which a society is organized into moieties. Malinowski criticized anthropologists like Rivers for failing to see that superficial social structure is the result of its "inner" structure:

The old theories of tribal dichotomy, the discussions about the 'origins' of 'phratries' or 'moieties' and of the duality in tribal subdivisions, never entered into the inner or differential foundations of the external phenomenon of halving. The recent treatment of the 'dual organization' by the late Dr. Rivers and his school suffers badly from the defect of looking for recondite causes instead of analyzing the phenomenon itself. The dual principle is neither the result of 'fusion' nor 'spitting' nor of any other sociological cataclysm. It is the integral result of the inner symmetry of all social transactions, of the reciprocity of services, without which no primitive community could exist. A dual organization may appear clearly in the division of a tribe into two 'moieties' or be almost completely obliterated — but I venture to foretell that wherever careful inquiry be made, symmetry of structure will be found in every savage society, as the indispensable basis of reciprocal obligations. (pp. 24–25)

We do no injustice to Malinowski to say that he maintained at this time that social structure may be stated as a system of rules according to which a given society ideally operates. The way in which natives actually obey or fail to obey the system must, of course, also be considered by the ethnographer, but this overt behavior of the natives is part of the "imponderabilia." A person's behavior in society cannot be understood by the ethnographer, Malinowski insisted, until he has made a very full observational record of the actual behavior of many people, and has made some attempt to enter into native life himself. Concerning his own attempts to enter into Trobriand life, Malinowski testified:

Out of such plunges into the life of the natives . . . I have carried away a distinct feeling that their behaviour, their manner of being . . . became more transparent and easily understandable than it had ever been before. (1922, pp. 21–22)

What Malinowski was saying, of course, is that by entering native life, the ethnographer himself begins to internalize a knowledge of the rules of the society that is, for all purposes, the same as that of the natives. He is able to "understand" the behavior of the natives for the simple reason that, in terms of his own internalized knowledge, he would behave the same way under the same circumstances. As to how this knowledge arises in the minds of the natives and of the ethnographer, Malinowski asserted simply that it develops spontaneously from living in the social milieu:

First of all, it has to be laid down that we have to study here stereotyped manners of thinking and feeling. As sociologists, we are not interested in what A or B may feel *qua* individuals, in the accidental course of their own personal experiences — we are interested only in what they feel or think *qua* members of a given community. Now in this capacity, their mental states receive a certain stamp, become stereotyped by the institutions in which they live, by the influence of tradition and folk-lore, by the very vehicle of thought, that is by language. The social and cultural environment forces them to think and feel in a definite manner. (p. 23)

It would have constituted a very simple step for Malinowski to have identified this internalized knowledge of society that every native carries with him in his mind with the objective of ethnographic research, but he apparently never made this step. As we can see from his tripartite schema for stating an ethnographic description, Malinowski left no room for stating the natives' internal knowledge of their society but only for the comments they could make explicit concerning their internal knowledge. This native commentary he called nothing more than "an ethnic peculiarity of [a] given society" (p. 22). In his later work, this notion of a system of internalized knowledge about society, of systems of beliefs, and so on, came to play a much less prominent role, although it never completely disappeared.

Malinowski had little to say about language as such in *Argonauts of the Western Pacific*, and what he did have to say is contained in the chapter, "The Power of Words in Magic — Some Linguistic Data."

There he remarked that the language of magical texts is not like ordinary language. Magical style, unlike ordinary narrative style, "does not serve to communicate ideas from one person to another; it does not purport to contain a consecutive, consistent meaning. It is an instrument serving special purposes, intended for the exercise of man's specific power over things, and its meaning, giving this word a wider sense, can be understood only in correlation to this aim" (p. 432). The important thing to realize in connection with this statement is that Malinowski's view of meaning in the ordinary sense is that it is arrived at, in sentences of ordinary language, by the concatenation of the meanings of the elements in the sentences in a consistent way. Malinowski held the traditional view that the order of words in sentences reflects the order of ideas in the mind, as can be seen from the remark immediately following the one just quoted:

It [the meaning of magical texts] will not be therefore a meaning of logically or topically concatenated ideas, but of expressions fitting into one another and into the whole, according to what could be called a magical order of thinking, or perhaps more correctly, a magical order of expressing, of launching words towards their aim. (p. 432)

In view of what Malinowski later claimed to be the nature of language, it is important to realize that in *Argonauts of the Western Pacific* he held a very traditional notion about the meaning of discourse, and he distinctly viewed the semantic properties of magical texts to be exceptional. Even so, Malinowski seemed to believe that the meaning of magical texts could be arrived at through rules of some sort, but that whatever these rules might be, they were different from the rules governing the meaning of ordinary discourse. Later in the chapter, Malinowski in fact discussed in some detail the linguistic nature of magical texts and made several observations concerning how one can come to understand them (pp. 451–452).

1.3 "The Problem of Meaning" (1923)

Malinowski's article "The Problem of Meaning in Primitive Languages" appeared just one year after the publication of *Argonauts of the Western Pacific*; yet the linguistic views expressed in it are radically different. The changes in his outlook may be summarized as follows. First, he exactly reversed his assertion in *Argonauts of the Western Pacific* that the language of magic is a special kind of language use. In the article he considered, rather, that the language of magic is an exemplification of the basic and primary use of language, and that the use of language to communicate ideas is special or derivative. Language in its primary function is, in his words, "to be regarded as a mode of action, rather than as *a countersign of thought*" (1923, p. 297). Viewed as a "mode of action" an utterance receives its meaning not from a logical concatenation of the ideas expressed by the words comprising it but from its relation to the situational context in which it occurs. Thus,

> But when we pass from a modern civilized language . . . to a primitive tongue, never used in writing, where all the material lives only in winged words, passed from man to man — there it should be clear at once that conception of meaning as *contained* in an utterance is false and futile . . . utterances and situation are bound up inextricably with each other and the context of situation is indispensable for the understanding of the words. Exactly as in the reality of spoken or written languages, a word without *linguistic context* is a mere figment and stands for nothing by itself, so in the reality of a spoken living tongue, the utterance has no meaning except in the context of situation. (p. 307)

This was not to say that language could not be used to communicate thought but that such use was derivative:

> The manner in which I am using it [language] now, in writing these words, the manner in which the author of a book, or a papyrus or a hewn inscription has to use it, is a very far-fetched and derivative function of language. (p. 312)

This statement represents a radical departure from the position Malinowski gave in *Argonauts of the Western Pacific*, but we may say that it was anticipated there. Already in the book Malinowski expressed serious concern over the problem of *translation*, especially the problem posed by the difficulty of translating magical texts. He found that he was unable to translate them meaningfully into English, using ordinary English words and relying on English patterns of meaning composition. To account for this discrepancy, Malinowski appealed to the notion that the Trobrianders had a "magical way of thinking or expressing" which correlated with their objectives in using magic. But there is no direct evidence for believing that the Trobrianders are thinking in some radically different way from the usual at the time of performing their magic. Consequently, it seems that Malinowski, to account for the discrepancy, concluded that it would be sufficient to observe exactly what the natives were *doing* while they were uttering their magical texts and to say that the meaning of these texts was precisely their correlation with this activity. In this case, the activity defines magical "contexts of situation." To obtain the meaning of utterances when expressed in mundane situations, Malinowski asserted that one need merely correlate the utterances with whatever human activity happens to be going on at the time. The language used in connection with typical daily human activities — fishing, hunting, cultivating, buying and selling, eating, greeting, instructing a child, gossiping around a campfire — derives its meaning, he argued, from the context of concurrent human activity.

Malinowski's argument in "The Problem of Meaning in Primitive Languages" is that the use of language which makes possible semantic interpretations of utterances in that language by considerations of contexts of situation is the primary use of language. There are two aspects to Malinowski's argument: (1) in primitive society, where there is no written language, no other use of language is possible, and (2) everyone in all societies learns language in this way. Concerning the second part of Malinowski's argument, we can cite the following remark as typical of his view of language learning:

The child *acts* by sound at this state [in his life], and acts in a manner which is both adapted to the outer situation, to the child's mental state and which is also intelligible to the surrounding adults. Thus the significance of sound, the meaning of an utterance is here identical with the active response to surroundings and with the natural expression of emotions. (p. 319)

In fact, Malinowski argued, the first set of contexts of situation that the child experiences are magical ones, where by magical contexts of situation he meant those in which the individual imagines that a word or expression has some direct influence on the situation:

The infantile experience must leave on the child's mind the deep impression that a name has the power over the person or thing which it signifies. We find thus that an arrangement biologically essential to the human race makes the early articulated words sent forth by children produce the very effect which these words *mean*. . . . This of course is not the statement of a child's conscious views about language, but it is the attitude implied in the child's behaviour. (pp. 320–321)

Written language, as we have seen, is the only kind of language for which a semantic interpretation cannot be supplied by a context of human activity, since there is none to correlate with it. Thus Malinowski committed himself to a position that distinguishes between men who can read and write and men who cannot — only the former have the capacity to express statements that have meaning independent of the context of situation in which they find themselves. As we shall see, Malinowski later renounced this position in favor of one which maintains that no man has this capacity.

Let us now examine the arguments that Malinowski put forth in support of his contention that the meaning of utterances is supplied by their correlation with concurrent human activity. He opened his argument by presenting a text in the Kiriwinian language together with a word-for-word translation of it into English, and observing that the translation makes very little sense:

In analysing it [the text], we shall see quite plainly how helpless one is in attempting to open up the meaning of a statement by mere linguistic means; and we hall be able to realize what sort of additional knowledge, besides verbal equivalence, is necessary in order to make the utterance significant. (p. 300)

One is immediately struck by Malinowski's tacit identification of the "linguistic means" at one's disposal for determining the meaning of the Kiriwinian text with the verbatim English translation of it. Unfortunately, Malinowski built the rest of his argument on the assumption of the validity of this identification; the next step in the argument is to show that the ethnographer, in order to determine what was really meant by the utterance, must look beyond the text itself to the human activity that was going on at the time the text was uttered. But, of course, the linguistic means at the ethnographer's disposal are not at all exhausted once he has found the verbatim translation of the text into English; rather he has just begun to use them. Malinowski's argument, it will be noted, betrays a curious ethnocentricity. Malinowski was not at all concerned here to account for how the natives might understand the text in question; rather he was asking how an outsider could arrive at an understanding of it.

Malinowski followed this part of his argument with a discussion of the meaning of a particular Trobriand sentence *boge laymayse*. He observed that he had particular difficulty in learning the meaning of this sentence but finally was able to conclude after some trial and error that it "means to a native 'they have already been moving hither' " (p. 304). In this discussion, Malinowski actually showed two things: (1) that it may be difficult for an outsider such as himself to learn the meaning of sentences in the native language, and (2) that it is nevertheless possible for a native to do so, independently of the contexts in which they might occur. Furthermore, he actually showed how it might be possible to characterize the meaning of the sentence just quoted in terms of the meanings of the lexical items comprising it, as follows:

In the Trobriand language . . . there is an adverbial particle *boge*, which, put before a modified verb, gives it, in a somewhat vague manner, the meaning of either a past or of a definite happening. The verb is moreover modified by a change in the prefixed personal pronoun. Thus the root *ma* (come, move hither) if used with the prefixed pronoun of the third singular *i* — has the form *ima* and means (roughly) *he comes*. With the modified pronoun *ay* — or more emphatical, *lay* — it means (roughly) *he came* or *he has come*. The expression *boge ayna* [sic] or *boge layma* can be approximately translated *he has already come*, the particle *boge* making it more definite. (p. 303)

We have discussed this example at rather tedious length because in it Malinowski carried out explicitly the semantic analysis of a Trobriand sentence in a way that was completely contradictory to his assertions about semantics in the rest of the paper. But this is not the only contradictory matter in the article. At one point Malinowski denied the assumption that the meaning of lexical items is "contained" in them, yet elsewhere he very explicitly referred to *the meaning* of lexical items (such as the Trobriand words *boge* and *ma*, and the English verb "run,") which he defined as "rapid personal displacement" (pp. 302–303).

In the remainder of his discussion, Malinowski simply took it for granted that it would be impossible to characterize the meaning of spoken utterances apart from the context of ongoing human activity; more specifically, that there is no way to characterize the meaning of utterances on the basis of internal considerations about the language alone. Rather, he asserted that the meaning of spoken utterances could always be determined by the context of situation. He failed, however, to consider a single one of the many objections that can immediately be raised against this notion. For example: how does the native speaker determine when two contexts are identical or partially alike? Not having the answer to this question, Malinowski is put in the position of a phonologist who asserts that he can give a phonological characterization of a language but cannot tell you when two utterances of the language are repetitions or partial repetitions of one another.[1] Or consider the question: How does the native speaker relate particular aspects of the situation to particular parts (or to the whole) of a given utterance? One can speculate only about the reasons why Malinowski failed to consider these objections, which, it must be admitted, if left unsolved are sufficient to vitiate the entire theory. It should be noted too that Malinowski's semantic theory takes as a fundamental notion the existence of fully integrated human perceptions concerning what is going on in the world. But to know how persons integrate their percep-

[1] This same argument is used by J. A. Fodor and J. J. Katz (1964, p. 13) against the ordinary-language philosophy notion of the "use theory of meaning." It is interesting to observe that the Oxford philosophers have maintained an outlook on semantics that bears great resemblance to that of Malinowski, Firth, and their linguistic followers, although there does not seem to have been much exchange between these two groups.

tions requires a much deeper understanding of human mental processes than that required to understand how semantic interpretations are assigned to sentences. Malinowski thus put himself in the unhappy position of attempting to account for one thing (the semantic interpretation of utterances) by something else (integration of sense perceptions and physiological state) incredibly more complicated.

It seems Malinowski simply assumed that it was obvious how people understand the nature of the context of situation given simply the situation itself. The gratuitousness of this assumption has been pointed out by Leach (1957, p. 128):

Actually Malinowski . . . postulated that the Trobriander was more rational than himself. Although he maintained that, for the Trobriander, there is a clear-cut division between the domain of knowledge and work and the domain of magic, he later confessed that 'I was not able to judge for myself where rational procedure ended and which were the supererogatory activities whether magical or aesthetic' (*Coral Gardens and Their Magic*, Vol. I, p. 460).

It should be clear that Malinowski in formulating his semantic theory was oblivious to the fatal objections that can immediately be raised against it. He furthermore put forward very strong claims about the explanatory power of his proposed semantic theory, in particular the assertion that it accounts for the way in which a language in a given culture develops its characteristic grammatical and semantic structure:

Each primitive or barbarous tribe, as well as each type of civilization has its world of meanings and the whole linguistic apparatus of this people — their store of words and their type of grammar — can *only* [emphasis mine] be explained in connection with their mental requirements. (1922, p. 309)

By "mental requirements" he meant here, presumably, the demands placed upon the mind by the range of possible contexts of situation that may be encountered in the given society. This passage is reminiscent of his earlier discussion in "Classificatory Particles" of a semantic theory that would account for the existence and character of certain grammatical facts in all languages on the basis of the structure of societies. Here he is asserting something stronger, namely, that a semantic theory in which the meaning of expressions is given by the context in which they occur accounts in some deep way for the nature of the total structure of all languages. However, the assertion was not supported by research into relevant material, and unfortunately Malinowski did not explore the question of how future research might proceed in order to examine its validity.

Our discussion of Malinowski's paper "The Problem of Meaning in Primitive Languages" has been concerned so far with his arguments in the first three sections of the paper. In section IV of the paper, he attempted to show how the meaning of utterances can be determined in three distinctly different types of context of situation. Those are (1) situations in which putatively speech interrelates directly with bodily activity that is, furthermore, culturally "significant"; (2) narratives, and (3) situations in which speech is used to fill, so to speak, a speech vacuum. He nowhere stated this to be an exhaustive classification of possible semantically relevant contexts of situations and, in fact, never raised the question of what would constitute an exhaustive classification.

Before going on to consider Malinowski's examples of each of these types, it must be pointed out that he believed that if a person was to know the semantic relevance of a particular context of situation, he must first have experienced it firsthand. One cannot, in his view, be taught by explanation or some other device how particular contexts define particular utterances.

To illustrate contexts of situation of type 1, Malinowski portrayed a typical Trobriand fishing scene, and asserted:

All the language used during such a pursuit is full of technical terms, short references to surroundings, rapid indications of change — all based on customary types of behaviour, well-known to the participants from personal experience. Each utterance is essentially bound up with the context of situation and with the aim of the pursuit, whether it be the short indications about the movements of the quarry, or references to statements about the surroundings, or the expression of feeling and passion inexorably bound up with behaviour, or words of command, or correlation of action. The structure of all this linguistic material is inextricably mixed up with, and dependent upon, the course of the activity in which the utterances are embedded. The vocabulary, the meaning of the particular words used in their characteristic technicality is not less subordinate to action. For technical language, in matters of practical pursuit, acquires its meaning only through personal participation in this type of pursuit. It has to be learned, not through reflection but through action.

Had we taken any other example than fishing, we would have reached similar results. The study of any form of speech used in connection with vital work would reveal the same grammatical and lexical peculiarities: the dependence of the meaning of each word upon practical experience, and of the structure of each utterance upon the momentary situation in which it is spoken. Thus the consideration of linguistic uses associated with any practical pursuit, leads us to the conclusion that language in its primitive forms ought to be regarded and studied against the background of human activities and as a mode of human behaviour in practical matters. . . . In its primitive uses, language functions as a link in concerted human activity, as a piece of human behaviour. It is a mode of action and not an instrument of reflection. (pp. 311–312)

This lengthy citation has been given to reveal both the absurd consequences of Malinowski's semantic notions and the true insights that he had concerning the meaning of words and utterances. Since Malinowski insisted that one cannot know the correlation between contexts of situation and utterances until one has experienced them together, it follows that in order to understand Trobriand fishermen while they fish, one must oneself be a Trobriand fisherman. If another Trobriander, who had never fished before, were for some reason invited along one day to observe the others he would not be able to understand a word they were saying — they might as well have been speaking English.

Another more devastating consequence of Malinowski's position is that at any given moment in his life a person is able to understand only a finite (in fact, extremely small) number of utterances in his own language. This consequence follows from the simple observation that man's finite life span limits him to only a finite number of experiences. The only way in which Malinowski is permitted to say that a person can indeed understand an infinite number of utterances of his language (and this, after all, is an empirical fact) is for him to state that a person understands any two utterances which occur in the same context of situation as complete synonyms. This is obviously an intolerable conclusion.

From the passage just cited, however, we can also see that Malinowski had an important insight into the nature of the meaning of particular words, namely, that their meaning is not given by the physical properties of their referents but rather by their function. In order to learn the functional meaning of such words, the use to which their referents are put must in some way be experienced. This insight is, of course, by no means Malinowski's discovery; the idea goes back at least to Aristotle's *De Anima*. In a sense, Malinowski's semantic theory resulted from pushing this insight to the extreme. He insisted that all words are functionally defined, and not only all words but all possible utterances in a language, and further that the meanings are so learned only by active experience and never by explanation or paraphrase. This is brought out clearly in the following remark:

Returning to the above examples of a group of natives engaged in a practical pursuit, we see them using technical words, names of implements, specific activities. A word, signifying an important utensil, is used in action, not to comment on its nature or reflect on its properties, but to make it appear, be handed over to the speaker, or to direct another man to its proper use. The meaning of the thing is made up of experiences of its active uses and not of intellectual contemplation. Thus, when a savage learns to understand the meaning of a word, this process is not accomplished by explanations, by a series of acts of apperception, but by learning to handle it. A word *means* [emphasis his] to a native the proper use of the thing for which it stands, exactly as an implement *means* something when it can be handled and means nothing when no active experience of it is at hand. Similarly a verb, a word for an action, receives its meaning through an active participation in this action. A word is used when it can produce an action and not to describe one, still less to translate thoughts. The word therefore has a power of its own, it is a means of bringing things about, it is a handle to acts and objects and not a definition of them. (pp. 321–322)

The second use of language for which Malinowski attempted to show how the meaning of utterances is given by contexts of situation is the narrative use. Narratives, Malinowski claimed, are associated with two different contexts of situation: the situation of the moment of narration and the situation referred to by the narrative. He did not consider the possibility of further regress — of narratives within narratives — but this was simply an oversight. Malinowski defined the context of situation of the moment of narration as being "made up of the respective social, intellectual and emotional attitudes of those present" (p. 312). But if so, then obviously it makes no sense to say that the meaning of narrative has anything to do with the context of situation of the moment of narration, for in what sense does the meaning of what is said depend upon the attitude of the listeners? Suppose one member of the audience falls asleep and another proceeds to daydream. Surely this would not affect the meaning of what is being said! It is clear, however, that Malinowski did not intend this either; he did not assert that the meaning of a narrative has anything to do with the situation of the moment of narration. Instead, he merely wished to show that narratives may have the effect of changing the social and emotional attitudes of the audience In other words, he was attempting to show how the *use* of language may be correlated with socially and emotionally characterized contexts, but not the *meaning* of what is said. This is certainly a less ambitious goal for a theory of context of situation to achieve. Yet, on further consideration of this case, even if narratives are to be considered "modes of social action," it is not the actual social effect that is significant but the intended effect on the part of the narrator. The actual narration may fail to achieve the social effect intended or it may achieve effects far beyond the initial expectations of the narrator. And while we may legitimately expect a high degree of correlation between what a storyteller says and his purposes in telling his story, it is clearly too much to suppose that we can predict in detail what he will say if we have advance knowledge of his intentions. It goes without saying that his intentions may change several times during the actual course of his narration.

The context of situation that, according to Malinowski, supplies the meaning of a narrative is the context referred to in the narrative in exactly the same way as in case 1:

. . . the words of a tale are significant because of previous experience of the listeners; and their meaning depends on the context of situation referred to. (p. 313)

Therefore the same objections which we raised against case 1 apply here in case 2.

Case 3 is a consideration of "the case of language used in free, aimless, social intercourse" (p. 313). Malinowski observed correctly that such use of language cannot be related in any way to any other ongoing human activity, so the question is: What context of situation supplies the meaning to utterances in this case? Malinowski identified it simply as

. . . just this atmosphere of sociability and . . . the fact of the personal communion of these people. But this is in fact achieved by speech, and the situation in all such cases is created by the exchange of words, by the specific feelings which form convivial gregariousness, by the give and take of utterances which make up ordinary gossip. (p. 315)

If this is the context of situation, however, then it certainly cannot be argued that the meaning of speech acts embedded in this context is supplied by it. If so, it would again be true that all instances of free social speech intercourse (which Malinowski called "phatic communion" [p. 315]) are synonymous. Instead of adopting this conclusion, Malinowski admitted that indeed the context of situation is unrelated to *the meaning* of utterances occurring in it:

A mere phrase of politeness . . . fulfils a function in which the meaning of its words is almost completely irrelevant. (p. 315)

Thus all that Malinowski asserted concerning the nature of "phatic communion" was simply that it is a context, more or less well defined, in which people are not particularly concerned with what they say or with what they mean by what they say, and that they speak simply to avoid having to remain silent. From this it follows, however, that in general it is impossible to predict what people will say or whether they will say anything from a knowledge of the context of situation. Curiously enough, it has been remarked that in situations in which men speak simply to avoid the embarrassment of having to remain silent, they resemble automata more than at any other time (Gardiner, 1951, pp. 43–44). We can remark only that if it is impossible to predict what men will say at the times when they most resemble automata — no matter what we know about the context of situation (including knowledge of the participants' complete past history and present physiological state) — how much more absurd it is to expect that we should be able to make such predictions when men are acting in their fullest human capacity.

This completes our investigation of section IV of "The Problem of Meaning in Primitive Languages." We have shown that in it Malinowski failed to prove that the meaning of utterances is in any way related to contexts of situation, and that he admitted as much where the context of situation is either that of narration or "phatic communion." We have seen furthermore that Malinowski failed to show that even his lesser goal, that of relating the use of language to context of situation, can be achieved.

We have already noted that Malinowski seems to have been convinced that it is speech itself, rather than the intentions behind speech acts, that determines social situations. However, considerations of actual social situations should quickly convince us that such is not the case. We may take as a simple example a social situation that Malinowski himself described in one of his ethnographic descriptions of Trobriand culture (1926, p. 78): a young man, an offended lover, publicly insults another party for an alleged crime with the purpose of setting public opinion so strongly against that party that he has no recourse but to commit suicide. Certainly, in this case what determined the social situation was not the actual insult that the young man hurled but his intentions in so doing. We can be quite certain that the one who made the public insult meditated beforehand on what he should say so as to make sure that a skeptical audience would be convinced of his case. The hearers certainly did not reach the conclusion, "the insulted party must commit suicide," simply upon hearing the speech. They arrived at the conclusion upon weighing the merit of the case as they perceived it, together with a determination of what the appropriate settlement of the matter should be.

Consider also the speech act that Malinowski quoted in section II of "The Problem of Meaning" in which a Trobriander boasted of his superior sailing prowess. The speech, Malinowski remarked, was intended to incite envy or admiration in his hearers, according to their relationship to him (1922, p. 301). What motivated the native to speak in this way was the desire not simply to obtain the outward signs of awe and admiration from his hearers but to gain evidence that those persons *thought* him to be awe-inspiring and powerful. The important determinants of social situations in which speech acts are prominent are, therefore, not the speech acts themselves but the participants' thoughts, both those of the speakers and those of the hearers. The matter has been well put in the Port-Royal *Logic*:

> It is not . . . the simple outward effects of the respect of men, separated from the consideration of their thoughts, which constitute the objects of love to the ambitious; they wish to command men, not automatons. (Arnaud, 1662, p. 71)

Section V of the paper is devoted to a discussion of infant psychology, which was designed to show that children acquire language as a mode of behavior rather than as an instrument to express thought. We have already commented on the crucial part that this assertion plays in Malinowski's whole argument (see p. 17 in this chapter). His argument that children acquire language as a mode of action consisted of the observation (1) that a child is endowed with arrangements for his total care thanks to his parents' instinctive concern for him, and (2) the best means that the child has for calling attention to his needs is by making noise, which, as language begins to develop in him, proves to be an efficient means for bringing about the amelioration of his conditions.

While these observations may be correct, as far as they go, it is certainly clear that they provide no basis for accounting for language acquisition; the very most that they can account for is that a child will develop a small number of arbitrarily chosen noises to designate particular discomforts, requirements, and so on. That Malinowski should have left out of his account any mention of a child's purely verbal intercourse with other people is quite surprising. Even the staunchest of contemporary behavioral psychologists, for example Skinner, attempt to account for language acquisition in these terms, and they at least make the assertion that a child is able to coin new speech acts *ad lib* and assign to them semantic interpretations by analogy with what he already knows. If this theory is far too weak to account for the speed and precision with which a language or a set of languages is learned by a child (cf. Chomsky, 1959), how much worse off are Malinowski's speculations! Malinowski furthermore seemed to be under the impression that into late childhood, human beings use language simply to acquire things or in conjunction with the handling and using of objects.[2] It is, however, impossible to reconcile this position with his own observation that seven-year-old Trobriand children often turned out to be excellent informants and could discuss intelligently complex matters of tribal culture:

I have had most valuable information on several points of view from boys and even girls of seven to twelve years of age. . . . Very often . . . they would talk and explain things with a surprising lucidity and knowledge about tribal matters. (1916, pp. 224–225 in Redfield, 1948)

Malinowski proceeded from this discussion of child language to a consideration of the language of primitive men through the astonishing suggestion that the language of primitive men is identical to child language in the sense just described. This identification is, however, in Malinowski's terms a perfectly natural one. Since the essential distinction between primitive and civilized men is the ability of the latter to read and write, and children in civilized society up to some age do not know how to do either, Malinowski's identification of primitive men with children of (civilized) society follows immediately.

Section VI, the final section of the paper, is devoted to a brief investigation of how the categories of universal grammar arise in the mind. Briefly, he contended that the universal categories, which he called "real categories," are reflections of universal human attitudes toward life and are brought out by the universally found conditions under which children grow up in the world:

Language in its structure mirrors the real categories derived from practical attitudes of the child and of primitive man to the surrounding world. The grammatical categories . . . are the reflection of the makeshift, unsystematic, practical outlook imposed by man's struggle for existence in the widest sense of the word. (1923, pp. 327–328)

It is not immediately clear from this citation that Malinowski considered these "practical attitudes of the child" to be innate attitudes or ones that he learns from his early experience. It would seem from his subsequent discussion that he considered them to be innate; he characteristically spoke of their "appearance" rather than of their "learning" (p. 332). Furthermore, since he considered that the universal categories are "identical for all human languages, in spite of the many superficial diversities" (p. 328), they must, in his view, arise from man's nature rather than from his experience.

---

[2] Thus, Malinowski (1923, p. 321) maintained, "Following the manner in which speech is used into the later stages of childhood, we find again that everything reinforces this pragmatic relation to meaning."

Malinowski wanted his assertion that the categories of universal grammar arise out of man's "attitude toward the world" to be taken as a denial of two other possible claims about their origin: (1) that they are derived from categories necessary for thought, and (2) that they have simply sprung up in the mind to serve as a basis for grammar construction alone. His argument against the first claim, however, is vitiated on the grounds that the position necessarily entails the identification of the categories of universal grammar with the categories of logic. His argument simply consisted of the remark that the categories of logic are "ill-adapted" to those of grammar (p. 327). Malinowski apparently missed the fact that grammarians who have maintained this claim generally have not made this identification but rather have stated that certain logical categories (such as predication, and the truth-function relations) form only a subset of the categories of universal grammar. Thus Malinowski's objection vanishes. Whether or not we should agree to accept the first claim depends ultimately upon our characterization of the human faculty of thinking, and on whether it can be shown that the categories of universal grammar are derived from this faculty or that both faculties spring from more "ultimate" sources.

We can have no dispute, however, with Malinowski's rejection of the second claim — accepting the first necessarily entails rejecting the second. Malinowski, of course, had other reasons for rejecting the second claim; he believed that there are certain aspects of nonlinguistic human behavior which make their appearance at various stages in childhood and which involve making categorizations that resemble in great detail the categories of universal grammar. The fact that this behavior can be explained only in terms of innate ability to categorize, which furthermore strongly resembles the categorizations found in universal grammar, was taken by Malinowski as evidence confirming the existence of the categories of universal grammar in the mind. The insight itself is quite profound, although his illustrative examples are not particularly exciting.

His first illustration involves the category that he called "crude substance." He maintained that this category underlies the universal grammatical category usually called "noun substantive" and a complex set of typical behavior of young children that makes itself manifest when the child begins to play with things and includes interests, fascination with detachable, holdable objects, and the tendency to be destructive, that is, to try to pull complex objects apart. He argued further that this attitude lasts throughout life and is especially pronounced in adult primitive men:

Their interest in animals is relatively greater than in plants; greater in shells than in minerals, in flying insects than in crawling ones. That which is easily detached is preferred. In the landscape, the small details are often named and treated in tradition, and they arouse interest, while big stretches of land remain without name and individuality. (p. 331)

Malinowski had less to say about the real category corresponding to the universal grammatical category of verb, and he argued that "the underlying real category appears later in the child's mental outlook, and it is less preponderant in that of the savage" (p. 332). The category is said to involve action, states of the body and human mood, to be associated with change in time, and "it lends itself to command as well as to indication and description" (p. 333). As to its extralinguistic correlates, Malinowski listed man's "great interest in all changes referring to the human being, in phases and types of human action, in states of human body and moods" (p. 333). These remarks are neither particularly convincing nor exciting, and the same can be said for the rest of his examples. Nevertheless, Malinowski's reason for searching out correlations between universal grammar and universal properties of extralinguistic behavior is the correct one, and it is certainly conceivable that further research in this area will uncover highly significant correlations of this type.

Grammatical categories considered universal by Malinowski include pronouns, adjectives, adverbs, conjunctions, and certain "cases" of nouns, including what he called appellative or nominative, possessive or genitive, objective or accusative, and "prepositional." The reason that this last case is universal, according to Malinowski, is that it is a universal human attribute to consider objects in spatial or temporal relationship to one another. If a particular language does not inflect nouns to indicate relationships like "in," "on," "before," and so on, then these relationships must be indicated by particles, such as English prepositions.

Section VI concludes with a discussion of what Malinowski called the "shifting of roots and meanings from one grammatical category to another" (p. 335). Malinowski argued that in very primitive languages there can be no grammatical processes that derive a word in one category from another word in another category, and more especially where the derivation makes no overt change in the form of the root. Such processes of derivation cannot take place in these languages, he insisted, because it presupposes the apparatus of "metaphor, of generalization, analogy and abstraction" (p. 335), and the existence of such apparatus in a language indicates that it is somewhat "developed."

What this development is supposed to be Malinowski did not say, but he did assert that to understand it one must know something about the "psychological and sociological processes of . . . semi-civilized communities" (p. 336). The reason that Malinowski wished to exclude such grammatical processes from primitive language was presumably his realization that they cannot be explained on the basis of his context of situation theory of language. Unfortunately, every known human language has an abundant supply of such grammatical processes, so that any attempt to correlate them with "sociological processes of semi-civilized communities" is doomed to failure.

1.4 *Coral Gardens and Their Magic* (1935)

Twelve years elapsed between the publication of "The Problem of Meaning in Primitive Languages" and the appearance of Malinowski's next, and final, extensive work on linguistic theory, *Coral Gardens and Their Magic*, Volume II. Although Malinowski's outlook evolved somewhat over that period, the change in his linguistic theory was considerably less than it had been between *Argonauts* and "The Problem of Meaning." The changes during the later period were mostly concerned with drawing out more fully the implications of his theory that the meaning of utterances is provided by the context of concurrent human activity.

We have already pointed out the curious ethnocentricity involved in the formulation of Malinowski's semantic theory, as it appeared in "The Problem of Meaning" (see earlier, p. 18). In his introduction to the second volume of *Coral Gardens*, he made this ethnocentricity explicit:

The theories here advanced will easily be seen to have originated in the actual difficulties of collecting, interpreting, translating and editing texts and terminologies. The approach presented has thus to a large extent been tested on the long and painful experience of learning a native language; on practice of speaking it, of gradually acquiring fluency and that intuitive understanding which enables us, as speaker, to handle the finer shades of meaning and, as hearer, to take part in the quick interchange between several people. (1935, p. xi)

In this book Malinowski introduced three new major ideas into his semantic theory, and all of them are related to the notion that the objective of linguistic analysis is to interpret actual texts in a foreign language in as satisfactory a manner as possible in the language of the ethnographer. The first of these is concerned with the context of linguistic data:

It will be obvious to anyone who has so far followed my argument that isolated words are in fact only linguistic figments, the products of an advanced linguistic analysis. The sentence is at times a self-contained linguistic unit, but not even a sentence can be regarded as a full linguistic datum. To us, the real linguistic fact is the full utterance within its context of situation. (p. 11)

The assumption that utterances in context are what constitute raw linguistic data is harmless enough, but what is not so harmless is the further assumption that the result of linguistic analysis constitutes a "figment" of the analysts' creation. The assumption amounts to a denial that language as such has any real status; all that exists is speech, and not simply speech but speech in contexts of situation.

The second new major idea concerns what Malinowski called the "range of meaning" of given words in the native vocabulary. (Notice that Malinowski did not consistently maintain his view on the fictitious status of words.) If a sound is used in two different contexts, it cannot be called one word — it must be considered as really two words that happen to be homophonous:

. . . in order to define a sound, we must discover, by careful scrutiny of verbal contexts, in how many distinguishable meanings it is used. Meaning is not something which abides within a sound; it exists in the sound's relation to the context. Hence if a word is used in a different context it cannot have the same meaning; it ceases to be one word and becomes two or more semantically distinguishable units. (p. 72)

It is not difficult to see the consequences of this remarkable view. For all practical purposes, every time a particular word is uttered it occurs in a novel verbal context, therefore no two utterance tokens of the same word ever have the same meaning, and conversely, it often happens that two different words (say *cat* and *dog*) occur as utterance tokens in the same context, therefore they must be considered synonymous in those contexts. Yet, for all its absurdity, the view follows quite logically from Malinowski's position concerning reality. Since the only reality is the utterance in context, the analyst can do nothing more than to collect and compare the utterances that he finds.

It will be noted that, in fact, Malinowski denied in *Coral Gardens* that there was any connection between mental categories and word classes in language. In the book he said that "we made an onslaught on the idea that native terminolgies represent native mental categories" (p. 73). Thus Malinowski retracted fully the fruitful idea he expressed in "The Problem of Meaning" that there is a deep underlying connection between mental categories and the categorial structure of the vocabulary.

Viewed in a different way, these two new ideas in *Coral Gardens* may be considered as consequences of Malinowski's decision to adopt the major tenets of behavioristic psychology (p. 236). Because of this adoption, he was of course forced to abandon his former views about the nature of culture in general that he expressed in *Argonauts*. This meant, in particular, he was obliged to maintain that the structure of society is somehow embodied in the actual behavior of its members and also to abandon the view that social structure is a psychological reality. In a remarkable passage Malinowski called the embodiment of social structure in actual behavior "meaning" and identified as the "real problem" of linguistics the characterization of such "meaning":

> By 'meaning' I understand a concept embodied in the behavior of the natives, in their interests, or in their doctrines. Thus the concept of magical force, for instance, exists in the very way in which they handle their magic. . . . Every magical ceremony is, in its essence, a handling of *mana*. . . . But the problem of ascertaining that, for instance, the concept of magical force is embodied in native behavior and in their whole theoretical approach to magic; and then of ascertaining that they certainly have no term for this concept and can only vicariously express it — this, in spite of its negative quality is the real problem of ethnographic linguistics. (p. 68)

The third new major notion in *Coral Gardens* is that the context of situation may enable one to "disambiguate" sentences that are semantically ambiguous. One simple illustration is the following:

> *I-woy-ye tau* means 'the man beats' or 'he (subject implied) beats the man'. The context gives the solution. (p. 32)

The realization that such potentially ambiguous sentences may in fact be understood in an unambiguous manner in certain circumstances was by no means a discovery on Malinowski's part. What is surprising, however, about his realization is that his semantic theory does not define the notion "potentially ambiguous sentence." This notion makes sense only if one supposes that meaning is a property of sentences, and that a sentence may have two or more distinct meanings connected with it. Within Malinowski's theory, on the other hand, no sentence should be ambiguous, since it can be correlated with at most only one context of situation at a time.

The citation given is not an isolated example. Another somewhat more involved example concerns the sentence *Bi-katumay-da, gala bi-giburuwa veyo-da, pela molu*, which occurred in one of Malinowski's Kiriwinian texts with the meaning "They might kill us as our kinsmen would not be angry because we would have been killed in famine" (p. 25). Malinowski remarked:

Now first of all this sentence is interesting because of its *essential ambiguity* [emphasis mine]. If the negative word *gala* were attached to the first verb the whole meaning would be opposite. It would run . . . 'They would never dare to kill us as our kinsmen would be angry because we had been killed in famine.' In fact to the European or Christian moral sense it would seem a much greater crime to murder a famished, exhausted man in times of national disaster and because he sought for a bare subsistence than to kill the same man because he was poaching. But the Trobrianders, obeying the stern law of necessity, have developed different rules. Our ethnographic knowledge, combined with the fact that the punctuation was indicated by the delivery enabled us to solve this ambiguity. (p. 42)

We may suppose that even if the delivery had not indicated the proper "punctuation" of the sentence, the sentence would still have been capable of disambiguation on the basis of ethnographic knowledge.[3] Here again Malinowski took for granted that potentially the sentence had two different semantic interpretations but without realizing that this should not be possible if his semantic theory were correct.

When we investigate the actual use that Malinowski made of the knowledge of context of situation to interpret particular utterances in the texts that he had collected, we discover that in fact he did not use it to supply their semantic interpretation at all. Rather, he used it to supplement his knowledge of their meaning, which he obtained independently of his knowledge of their contextual setting. Not only did he use knowledge about context of situation to disambiguate sentences, he used it also to supply antecedents for anaphorically selected pronouns, and to determine the exact reference of deictic pronouns. Even more convincing evidence that Malinowski did not actually attempt to determine the meaning of utterances from a knowledge of their setting is the fact that he was not at all hesitant to supply possible contexts of situation for particular texts. Certainly if the meaning of a text really depended upon the context in which it occurred, and was unintelligible apart from that context, it would in principle be impossible to speculate about the contexts in which a particular text could occur, given just that text itself. Yet, Malinowski felt perfectly free to do so:

Take, for example, the second text in our collection . . . *which on the face of it* [emphasis mine] is merely a definition of certain terms. . . . Let us see . . .

[3] Malinowski here seems to have abandoned his view that the context of situation is simply the context of ongoing human activity and to have replaced it with the view that the context of situation is instead the "context of culture," the total cultural setting of the speech act. But in so doing, the notion of context of situation is emptied of any significance that it had for semantics under his earlier view. As this particular example illustrates, the only possible relevance that the context of culture can have semantically is to disambiguate sentences that are inherently ambiguous semantically.

whether this text can naturally be placed within some normal context of native life. (p. 49)

We remarked earlier (p. 15) that between *Argonauts of the Western Pacific* and "The Problem of Meaning in Primitive Languages" Malinowski moved from a position where he treated the "magical" use of language as exceptional to one where he maintained that the "scientific and literary" use of language in civilized society was derivative — this being the only use of language to express thought independently of context of situation. In *Coral Gardens and Their Magic* Malinowski made the final step: he declared there that even literary and scientific language is not the expression of thought, but its meaning is also given by correlation with context of situation:

And it seems to me that, even in the most abstract and theoretical aspects of human thought and verbal usage, the real understanding of words is always ultimately derived from active experience of those aspects of reality to which the words belong. The chemist or the physicist understands the meaning of his most abstract concepts ultimately on the basis of his acquaintance with chemical and physical processes in the laboratory. Even the pure mathematician, dealing with that most useless and arrogant [sic!] branch of his learning, the theory of numbers, has probably had some experience of counting his pennies and shillings or his boots and buns. In short, there is no science whose conceptual, hence verbal, outfit is not ultimately derived from the practical handling of matter. I am laying considerable stress on this because, in one of my previous writings ["The Problem of Meaning"], I opposed civilised and scientific to primitive speech, and argued as if the theoretical uses of words in modern philosophic and scientific writing were completely detached from their pragmatic sources. This was an error, and a serious error at that. Between the savage use of words and the most abstract and theoretical one there is only a difference of degree. Ultimately all the meaning of all words is derived from bodily experience. (p. 58)

Despite the absurdity of the conclusion, there is an important true insight on Malinowski's part that underlies it. This insight is that for a man to be able to formulate certain concepts in his mind (and/or to be able to express them in words) he requires certain appropriate experience in the world. Thus, for example, for a man to understand such geometrical concepts as "things equal to the same thing are equal to each other," he must presumably have had sometime in his life experience with measuring properties of objects, such as, perhaps, length or weight. The flaw in Malinowski's argument is that he considered the relationship between the physical experience and the derived concepts to be a direct one.[4]

[4] This argument is essentially that presented by Descartes in reply to a position very much like Malinowski's; cf. Descartes (1647, pp. 442–444). I wish to thank Professor Chomsky for pointing this argument out to me.

In conclusion, a comment is in order concerning Malinowski's espousal of behavioral psychology as the basis for his theory of culture and of language. It turns out that since Malinowski never really gave up his earlier belief that the system of culture constitutes a psychological reality, there exists a real contradiction in his own writing at this time concerning the nature of culture. On the one hand, in accordance with behavioristic tenets, he argued that individuals are "molded" gradually by their experience in society:

. . . the influence of culture — that is, of all the institutions found within a community, of the various traditional mechanisms such as speech, technology, mode of social intercourse — this influence works on the individual by a gradual process of moulding. By this process of moulding I mean the effect of traditional cultural modes and norms upon the growing organism. In one way the whole substance of my theory of culture . . . consists in reducing Durkheimian theory to terms of Behavioristic psychology. (p. 236)

On the other hand, he consciously maintained that social structure is a psychological reality, in accordance with his own earlier views, so that, if you will, he failed in his enterprise of "reducing" his theory to the terms of behavioristic psychology:

Magic happens in a world of its own, but *this world is real to the natives* [emphasis mine]. It therefore exerts a deep influence on their behaviour and consequently is also real to the anthropologist. The situation of magic — and by this I mean the scene of action pervaded by influences and sympathetic affinities, and permeated by *mana* — this situation forms the context of spells. It is created by native belief, and this belief is a powerful social and cultural force. (p. 215)

1.5 Conclusion

In evaluating the influence of Malinowski's views about language, and in particular about semantics, on J. R. Firth and the London school, it is important to realize that it is only his views expressed in 1935 that had any effect. Consider, for example, how the notion "context of situation" was adopted by Firth. For him, the notion did not mean, as it did for Malinowski in 1923, the context of human activity concurrent with, immediately preceding, and following the speech act but rather the whole cultural setting in which the speech act is embedded, which was also Malinowski's position in 1935 (see also footnotes 1 and 3 in Chapter 3).

It is only the earlier ideas of Malinowski's, however, that appear to be based on any sort of profound insight. In particular, we may cite the ideas (1) that social structure is a psychological and, hence, not a directly observable reality, and that behavior can only be understood in terms of it; (2) that functional definitions of certain words are important in semantics and may be learned through active participation in the proper use of designated objects; and (3) that the categories of universal grammar must underlie categorizations implicit in nonlinguistic human behavior. In view of the scope of these insights, the severe judgment of a contemporary British anthropologist that "the abstract theoretical writings of Malinowski are not merely dated, they are dead" (Leach, 1957, p. 120) is simply false. However, the high esteem that Malinowski currently enjoys in the eyes of the London school is not based on a recognition of the value of these ideas but rather on the fact that he held notions such as that the meaning of utterances is given by their correlation with the context of situation; and these, as we have shown, not only can be proved false but were not consistently maintained by him.

2. The Early Views of J. R. Firth

In this chapter we shall consider Firth's papers in linguistics up to the time of his appointment to the Chair in General Linguistics at the University of London.[1] It will be instructive to compare the central ideas of this period with those of his later period, discussed in Chapter 3, when the London school was formed under his influence. It will be one of the objectives of this chapter to indicate the relationship of the ideas expressed in Firth's earlier writings to those of Malinowski and Daniel Jones, and to compare these ideas, at least with respect to phonology, to the notions current in American linguistics during the same period.

The single most important notion in Firth's early writings is that of context. One might say that Firth took the current notions of phonological, morphological, and lexical contexts, which were already well established in linguistics, added the Malinowskian notion of context of situation, and devised a view of language that may be regarded as an arrangement of contexts, each one serving as an environment for the elements or units at each of various "levels." Firth called these levels phonetic, lexical, morphological, syntactic, and semantic; the elements on each of these levels he called phonemes, words, morphemes, syntactic categories, and semantic categories; and the contexts he called phonological, lexical, morphological, syntactic, and situational (1935a, p. 27 in 1957c). Firth made no serious attempt to define any of these levels

---

[1] Most of Firth's work that we shall make reference to in this chapter has been reprinted in Firth, 1957c. His two early popular books, *Speech* (1930) and *The Tongues of Men* (1937), have been reprinted in Firth, 1964.

37

rigorously, and paid relatively little attention to any of them except the phonetic and the semantic levels. In particular, he made no attempt to arrange these levels systematically with respect to each other, except to note the following relationships among them:

1. Phonemes can only be studied in relationship to words. This position is taken directly from Jones;[2] what this meant for Firth was that the phonetic context relevant to the study of phonology is limited to the sounds contained within the units on the lexical level. External sandhi was thus excluded as a phonological problem for Firth at this time.[3]

2. If pairs of phonemes show a consistent relationship on the lexical, morphological, or syntactic levels, this, according to Firth, constitutes evidence that their differentiae are significant phonological features of the language. When a simple phonological opposition of this sort happens to be the only overt indication of an actual lexical, morphological, or syntactic opposition, then according to Firth, the particular phonemes have "major function" (1935*b*, p. 37, 1935*c*, p. 49, both in 1957*c*). On occasion, Firth used his knowledge of major function patterns to decide what the phonemes are in particular contexts in particular languages. Thus, the intervocalic Tamil sound [ɽ], a retroflexed flapped *d*, was said to represent the Tamil phoneme *ṭ*, because it stands in relation to phonemic *ṭṭ* [ʈʈ] in a major function in precisely the same way as do *t* to *tt*, *c* to *cc*, *ḷ* [ɭ] to *ḷḷ*, and so on. Firth gave examples such as the pair *paṭu* [paɽu] "I endure" versus *paṭṭu* [paʈʈu] "enduring," and so on, as manifesting the syntactic role of the opposition of single consonants to geminate consonants in Tamil (1935*c*, p. 49 in 1957*c*). Firth did not, however, give himself free rein in using syntactic information of this sort to help determine the optimal phonological analysis of languages, especially where it would lead him to identify phones as members of phonemes having sounds bearing little phonetic similarity to other members of the phoneme. Unfortunately, he never

[2] Thus Daniel Jones's well-known definition of the phoneme as "a family of sounds in a given language which are related in character and are used in such a way that no one member ever occurs in a word in the same phonetic context as any other member" (Jones, 1950, p. 10).

[3] This contention is supported by the observation that no such examples were discussed by Firth during his early period. Compare Jones's statement concerning the restriction "in a word" in his definition of the phoneme given in ftn. 2: "To extend the definition to cover word-groups or sentences would greatly complicate matters. At the best it would increase the number of phonemes in some languages; it might even be found to render the elaboration of any consistent theory of phonemes impossible, since variations of sound at word junctions may take so many forms" (Jones, 1950, p. 10).

made clear the constraints he was operating under. He seemed to admit "partial phonemic overlapping," as the following remark would indicate:

It so happens that intervocalic *kk* [in Malayalam] sounds rather like initial *k* and intervocalic *k* rather like g. (1936, p. 71 in 1957c)

In more complicated situations, however, Firth kept closer to the phonetic ground. Thus, for example, he argued that the vowels of the modern Sanskritic languages of India cannot be paired into a long and a short series, because besides the simple pairing of [ə] and [a] in major function, [ɪ] is paired with both [i] and [e] and [ʊ] is paired with both [u] and [o]. He quoted, as an illustration of the pairings, the Urdu passive forms [pɪsna] and [cʰɪdna], which are related to the active forms [pisna] and [cʰedna], respectively. Firth failed to consider as a possible phonemicization [i] as representing *ii*; [e] as representing *ai*; [ɪ] as representing *i*; [u] as representing *uu*; [o] as representing *au*; [ʊ] as representing *u*; [a] as representing *aa*, and [ə] as representing *a*. This solution permits the active and passive forms of the verb that Firth quoted to be related by a rule which in the passive voice deletes the first vowel of a two-vowel sequence in initial syllables of verbal roots.

Firth's concept of "major function," it should be noted, was certainly no new idea; although he acknowledged no sources for it, it corresponds closely to Sapir's or Bloomfield's or Boas's notion of internal modification. A tantalizing question is the extent to which Firth recognized that it was phonological *features*, rather than phonemes, which stood in opposition to one another in major function.[4] Firth was personally acquainted with Trubetzkoy (1948a, p. 124 in 1957c), and so was well acquainted with the work of the Prague school, but generally the ideas of this school seemed to have had little influence on him.

3. Forms that are ambiguous on one level are not necessarily ambiguous on another, and Firth seems to have realized to some extent that a hierarchy is imposed on his levels by this fact. Thus the form *bɔ:d* "board" on the phonetic level is "functionally ambiguous." By

[4] Some indication is provided by a handful of English examples, presented by Firth in "Technique of Semantics." There he recognized explicitly the "neutralization" of voicing in the English plural and past-tense suffixes, but only after stops and fricatives. After nasals, liquids, and vowels he maintained that the voicing of sibilants and stops is distinctive, citing for example the minimal pair *wins* and *wince*. He suggested as a possible spelling reform (tongue-in-cheek?) the representation of these words as *winns* and *wins*, respectively, commenting further that English spelling is not entirely absurd for keeping numerous homophones orthographically distinct. He also mentioned such examples as *wreath* and *wreathe* in which voicing of the final fricative indicates whether the item is a noun or a verb (1935a, pp. 23–24 in 1957c).

appeal to morphology, however, it may be determined whether the form is either an uninflected noun, an uninflected verb, or the "*d-form*" of a verb *bɔ:*. Similarly, the still ambiguous noun (on the morphological or lexical levels) may be resolved in specific contexts of situation, the contexts on the level of semantics. The semantic functions of the noun may be determined:

(1) *positively* by the use of the words in relation to the rest of the situational context, and (2) *negatively* by what is termed *contextual elimination*. The presence of a chess-board might eliminate a commercial board or a board of studies. (1935*a*, p. 26 in 1957*c*)

Firth defined "meaning" as the relationship between an element at any level and its context on that level. Thus, the meaning of any sentence consisted of the following five parts:

1. The relationship of each phoneme to its phonetic context, that is, the other phonemes in the word of which it is a part.

2. The relationship of each lexical item to the others in the sentence.

3. The morphological relations of each word, and perhaps also the relationship of each morpheme to every other word containing that morpheme (something like Saussure's notion of *rapports associatifs*).

4. The sentence type of which the given sentence is an example. Since Firth wrote practically nothing about syntax at any time during his life, one cannot determine by inspection of his printed work what the state of his ideas about syntax at that time actually was. Indeed, the following remark, taken from *Speech*, seems to indicate quite clearly that he held rather a dim view of syntax: "That Meillet should find it possible to compare our 'grammar' with that of Chinese only serves to show once more the unreality of grammar. The syntactical inter-relations of words is not nearly so important as word groupings and the relations between phonetic habits and contexts of experience." (1930, p. 190 in 1964)

5. The relationship of the sentence to its context of situation (1935*a*, p. 26 in 1957*c*)

Firth did little with the first four of these elements of the meaning "spectrum" during this early period. We shall return to consider his development of the notion of context of situation later after a discussion of his phonological ideas during this period.

In his earliest papers, "The Word 'Phoneme' " and "The Principles of Phonetic Notation in Descriptive Grammar," he defined the "phoneme" as a "functional unit" that consists of sounds which appear in nonoverlapping phonetic contexts in words:

One of the functional phonetic units of Tamil, for example, is something which is not *p*, *t*, or *pp*, or *tt*, or even *kk*, but variously *k*, *g*, *c*, *ç*, *x*, ɣ (I.P.A.), according to context. This kind of functional phonetic unit has been termed a *phoneme*. Six alternant *k*-phones have been selected from a very large number, because they are clearly distinguishable by the most stubborn ear. As an illustration of what is meant by a phoneme, we may take the Tamil *k*-phoneme above. The alternant phones k_1, k_2, k_3, k_4, k_5, k_6 necessarily occur under the conditions x_1, x_2, x_3, x_4, x_5, x_6, which are directly observable and definable in one style of speech of a certain type of speaker from a certain place, and can therefore be represented by the sign *k*. . . . In Tamil, therefore, the *k*-sign represents something used habitually in a variety of phonetic contexts, in which other 'sounds' or phonemes may also be used. (1934*b*, pp. 3–4 in 1957*c*; cf. also 1930, pp. 156–163 in 1964)

The phonological theory embodied in this remark is simply orthodox Daniel Jones phonemics. Jones, in fact, used this very example from Tamil (with credits to Firth) as an illustration of "the grouping of several quite distinct sounds into single phonemes" (1950, p. 22).

Very shortly afterward, however, Firth developed a much more cautious approach to phonological analysis involving a further restriction on what may constitute conditioning environments as well as the Jonesian restriction to intraword context. The new restriction involved defining two new notions: "specific" phonetic contexts and "general" phonetic contexts. To illustrate what Firth meant by distribution of sounds in specific contexts, we may quote:

. . . it will be seen that in the context *bi*:*d*, *i*: is used as distinct from fifteen other possible substitution counters, in *pul*, *u* is used in contra-distinction from eleven other phonemes, in *hɔd*, the use of ɔ is dependent on the potential use of the other twelve alternatives. (1935*b*, p. 37 in 1957*c*)

By comparing these specific contexts with one another, Firth said that he could arrive at a "general" context — call it *CVC* — in which twenty-one possible terms, or phonemes, can occur in the position marked *V*. In another general context *CV* only eighteen phonemes can occur in the position marked *V*, and so on (1935*b*, p. 37 in 1957*c*). The restriction that Firth introduced in phonemic analysis was that phonemes could only be defined for general contexts and not for the whole class of words of the language. The allophones of each phoneme of each general context are those sounds which are contextually defined within the class of specific contexts comprising the general context. Phonemes occurring in two different general contexts, or even in two different positions in the same general context, can definitely not be considered comparable with one another. Firth first enunciated this principle in his paper at the Second International Congress of Phonetic

Sciences in 1935 and based it on two examples, one from Hindi, and the second from Marathi:

> But it is only in certain general contexts that all forty alternances or substitutions [of plosives] are possible; e.g. medially or intervocalically, so that I should hesitate to make any general statement about the function or value of any one term in the language as a whole apart from a more or less determined [or general] context. Whereas *t* in intervocalic position is one of forty plosive terms in that context, in initial position it is one of twenty. . . . If you like, initial *t* is a different 'phoneme' from intervocalic *t*, the conventions of position differentiating them in the notation. (1935*c*, p. 48 in 1957*c*)

And:

> In initial position only two nasal consonants can be used, *n* and *m*. In final position there is a three-term nasal alternance, but immediately preceding another consonant, especially stops, only one is possible, the nasal homorganic with the following consonant. . . . The actual mechanism and act of utterance of *n*, for example, in each of the three cases would be different. . . . Though writing them with the same symbol on practical phonetic grounds, I should not identify them in any other way. That they are the same 'phoneme' is the very last thing I should say. (p. 51)

If made explicit, Firth's newly defined elementary phonological unit (at about this time, it seems, Firth stopped using the term "phoneme" as a technical term), is precisely the same thing as W. F. Twaddell's macrophoneme as defined in his 1935 monograph *On Defining the Phoneme*; and it is remarkable to note the similarity of their arguments for justifying the adoption of this new phonological entity. Twaddell's argument can be compared directly with Firth's just given:

> By taking all the articulatory ranges within which significant differentiation occurs in the language, we can construct the maximal phonological system of the language. But in nearly all languages, that potential maximum of differentiation is not uniformly realized. There are systematic gaps, i.e. there are cases of less than maximal differentiation within a given articulatory range. These systematic gaps are just as much a part of the phonological system as are the maximal differentiations. . . . For many linguists, it appears, the phoneme functions as a unit to be represented by a symbol in a so-called phonetic transcription. It appears that the unit these linguists require cannot sufficiently take into account either phonological or phonemic facts; it would clarify the issue if these units might be called 'graphemes', 'transcribemes', or even 'letters'. For I know of no earlier phoneme definition which does not achieve transcriptional sanctions by violence to essential phonological relations and palpable phonetic fact. (1935, p. 73 in Joos, 1957)

The similarity of Firth's position to that of Twaddell has rarely been noted; Robins has pointed it out (1961, p. 198), but he compared

Firth's later theory of prosodic analysis not his phonological theory of 1935 with Twaddell's position.[5]

The general contexts, with respect to which Firth's new "phonemes" were defined, all turn out to be what is generally called syllable types, defined with respect to position within words. Typical general contexts for Firth were, then, word-initial and final, intervocalic, closed syllable, open syllable, and so on. He was apparently of the opinion that consonant clusters (except when they occur across a syllable division) are always to be regarded as units, or phonemes in his new sense:

Consonant groups, such as *st, str, sp, spl, sk, skr*, in initial position in English, are best regarded as group substituents and no attempt should be made to identify the function of the letter '*t*' (here part of a digraph or trigraph) with that of a similar letter used in another context. (1936, p. 73 in 1957c)

Firth meant this to be taken as a serious proposal governing phonological analysis, but it can easily be seen that in many cases it may lead to the introduction of complexities in phonological statements. In classical Greek, for example, if initial clusters were considered to be units of their own, then the form *bállō* "I throw" would be represented by Firth *bállō*, whereas *blépō* "I see" would be represented, say, as *Bépō*, where *B* symbolizes initial *bl*. But the middle aorist participle of *bállō*, namely *blémenos*, would also have to be represented as *Bémenos*, thus missing the obvious fact that the initial cluster in the participle arises by the apocope of the initial vowel, and consists of the *b* and the *l* of the underlying verb root. And Firth's description would still require a rule stating that phonological *B* was pronounced [bl]! In this connection, it is worth noting another comment of Firth's, that "the Arabic and Indian alphabets are such that they have developed either initial, medial or final forms, or special compound letters. Such specialization of form may even be justified by abstract general phonetic theory . . ." (p. 70).

Firth's analysis of the monosyllable in a Hunanese dialect of Chinese (Firth and Rogers, 1937, pp. 76–91 in 1957c) is the only descriptive work in which he attempted to use his new phonological approach to any degree. It is immediately clear upon investigation of his analysis that

[5] Firth's only published discussion of Twaddell's work is the following, contained in a footnote in "Technique of Semantics": "That the general theory of the phoneme is in the melting-pot has been shown by W. Freeman Twaddell in his dissertation *On defining the Phoneme*. . . . It is all rather like arranging a baptism before the baby is born. In the end we may have to say that a set of phonemes is a set of letters" (1935a, p. 21 in 1957c).

he was led to introduce a number of complexities into his statement, several of which have already been pointed out by Einar Haugen in his review of Firth's *Papers*. Haugen pointed out, for instance, that Firth's failure to identify word initials *y* and *w* with the *y* and *w* that follow a word-initial consonant leads to complexity in stating the conditions on other allophonic variations:

> In Chinese /y/ is a phoneme in /ya/ but a prosody in /hya/, described as 'yotization'. Yet his description of the alophonic effects of /y/ on following vowels shows that it is the same whether it is a consonant or a prosody (cf. the description of following /u/ as a 'close centralized vowel with slight friction' after /y/ and in 'yotized syllables' [p.] 82). Because the postinitial /y/ contrasts with /w/ only, Firth regards it as having a different function and assigns it to the level of the syllable. But the argumentation is far from compelling. (1958, p. 501)

Of course, Haugen's objection to Firth's analysis is not entirely right as it stands, because he would substitute for it an analysis that obscures the fact that after consonants, "/y/ contrasts with /w/ only"; what is required is a phonological representation that indicates those features shared uniquely by word-initial and postconsonantal *y* (to enable the simplest statement of the allophonic variation of *u*, and so on) *and* that clearly shows in the representation that after consonants *y* contrasts only with *w*.

Haugen also pointed out that because Firth chose to designate two different syllable types (and hence two different general contexts) — those with "closing nasalization," that is, nasalization of the final vowel of the syllable, and those that are closed with a fully articulated alveolar nasal — he missed an obvious simplification in his analysis. The facts are that in syllables with closing nasalization, only the mid-vowels *o*, ɤ, and *e*, and the diphthong *ao* may appear, while in syllables closed with a fully articulated nasal consonant, only the non-mid-vowels *i*, *a*, and *u* may occur. Haugen made the obvious suggestion — since closing nasalization and final articulated nasal are in complementary distribution with respect to the preceding vowel — why not treat them as allophonic variants, thus reducing the number of syllable types to one in which, furthermore, all of the vowels of the language are permitted to occur (p. 500)? A similar case in which Firth refused to apply the principle of complementary distribution is concerned with Burmese. Firth noted that in a particular context voiceless stops occur to the exclusion of voiced stops, while in another context only the voiced stops appear, and commented: "It seems to me quite unnecessary and probably erroneous to postulate relations between the stops in these two utterly different contexts. The question of what letters we shall use in Romanic orthography is another matter altogether" (1936, p. 64 in 1957c). By adopting this position on complementary distribution, of course, Firth was able to sidestep contemporary live issues concerning that principle, for example, whether the sound after the *s* in *stick* is to be identified with the phoneme *t* or *d* (p. 72), and whether ŋ and *h* are members of the same phoneme in English (p. 74).

This concludes our discussion of Firth's early phonological ideas. As we shall see in the next chapter these ideas led quite naturally into Firth's one major phonological idea of the later period, prosodic analysis. There is also a genuine parallel between Firth's development of phonology in this way and the simultaneous development in America of the notions "distributional analysis" of phonemes and of "long components" out of Twaddell's macrophoneme idea.

Returning now to Firth's semantic ideas, the central notion for him, as for Malinowski, was that of context of situation. But in the same way as Malinowski in 1935, Firth defined context of situation as including the entire cultural setting of speech and the personal history of the participants rather than as simply the context of concurrent human activity:

> The central concept of the technique here sketched is the context of situation, in which, in a sense, whole stretches of personal biography, and cultural history are involved, and in which past, present, and future all meet. (1935a, p. 18 in 1957c)

However, it seems Firth realized the impossibility of using this notion to provide semantic interpretation of sentences, because practically nothing can be said about it in any relevant way. He recognized that sentences were "infinitely various" (p. 28). So, in the very same paragraph in which he expressed this recognition, he introduced a new notion, that of "typical" context of situation, which is at least not subject to the objection that nothing systematic can be said about it.

By a typical context of situation, Firth meant that aspect of the social situation in which people happen to find themselves at a given moment — which determines the social roles each of them are obliged to play. Since for any individual the total number of social roles he must play is finite, the number of typical contexts of situation that he will encounter in life will also be finite. Firth then asserted that semantics is not the study of speech in contexts of situation of the Malinowskian type but rather of speech in typical contexts, that semantics is properly the study of those speech styles which are appropriate to specific social roles that individuals play:

Speech is not the 'boundless chaos' Johnson thought it was. For most of us the roles and lines are there, and that being so, the lines can be classified and correlated with the part and also with the episodes, scenes and acts. Conversation is much more of a roughly prescribed ritual than most people think. Once someone speaks to you, you are in a relatively determined context, and you are not free just to say what you please. We are born individuals. But to satisfy our needs we have to become social persons, and every social person is a bundle of roles or *personae;* so that the situational and linguistic categories would not be unmanageable. Many new categories would arise from a systematic observation of the facts. (p. 28)

Semantics, then, was defined as the classification of utterances of a language into the typical contexts of situation for which they might be appropriate. Whether or not we consider this to be a worthwhile task, or even a possible one in any significant sense, it should immediately be apparent that such "semantics" has nothing whatever to do with the meaning of sentences in the ordinary sense of the word.

This fundamental inadequacy has, however, been recognized by members of the London school; Palmer has pointed out that there is no linguistic use for the notion of context of situation (in the sense just defined) except for the purpose of delimiting various styles of speech (1958, p. 237). He has pointed out quite emphatically the irrelevance of the notion of context of situation for the study of meaning:

Statements about context of situation may claim greater objectivity, and it might be theoretically supposed that all utterances could though in a very complex statement, be ultimately accounted for in terms of the situations in which they are employed and the way in which they are expressed in these sentences. In practice, however, only a tiny fraction of what is usually meant by meaning, appears to be statable in terms of context of situation. (p. 236)

Firth went further than to say simply that for the proper study of sentences they should be classified according to the typical contexts of situation for which they are appropriate. He maintained that the class of utterances appropriate to each context is an entity of its own, a separate "language" if you will, having no relationship with any other class of utterances. As a consequence, he came to view the notion "unity of language" as a misconception:

The multiplicity of social roles we have to play . . . involves also a certain degree of linguistic specialization. Unity is the last concept that should be applied to language. . . . There is no such thing as *une langue une* and there never has been. (1935a, p. 29 in 1957c)

As with many of Firth's pronouncements, this one is open to a considerable latitude of interpretation. Under the most favorable interpretation, Firth is simply saying that in some sense the language of baby talk is different from ordinary discourse, and this again is different from the language of legal documents, but even here to say that "unity is the last concept that should be applied to language" is highly misleading. A less favorable interpretation makes Firth out to say that the expression *Good day!* when uttered as a greeting is completely unrelated to the same *Good day!* when uttered as a farewell, and so on for countless such instances. The extreme form of this position, that each language act (speech, conversation, and so on) is to be studied in and of itself without reference to any other, has apparently been taken recently by R. M. W. Dixon; compare Langendoen (forthcoming *a*).

Firth's decision to deny ontological status to the notion "language" is, however, easy to understand as soon as it is realized that his "Technique of Semantics," in which it was first expressed, was written as a reply to Sir Alan Gardiner's book *The Theory of Speech and Language* (1951; first ed., 1932). Gardiner developed in considerable detail the Saussurean notion of language, as opposed to speech, as the subject matter of linguistics. The decision, obviously, destroys Gardiner's distinction between speech and language — only the former exists. Indeed, as it may be seen clearly from Firth's later writings, he was anxious to demolish all Saussurean dualisms such as *langue/parole*, *signifiant/signifié* and, beyond these, such dualisms as thought/expression.[6] He viewed this wish as being in complete agreement with the "prevailing ideas" of positivism and behavioral psychology of his times — this in spite of his later curious disclaimer about not being antimentalistic (1951*b*, p. 225 in 1957*c*) — as the following citation clearly shows:

Nevertheless a pragmatic functionalism seems to me to lead to much clearer definition, and to the statement and explanation of facts, without having to postulate a whole body of doctrine in an elaborate mental structure such as is derived from de Saussure. The description and explanation of our facts by the simple process of contextualization, the distinction between minor and major functions into morphological, syntactical, lexical, semantic, etc., seems to me fundamentally sound in the present state of our knowledge and for future progress in harmony with prevailing ideas. (1935*b*, p. 36 in 1957*c*)

In adopting a more or less behavioristic outlook, Firth took over completely Malinowski's ideas concerning the nature of language acquisition by children, ideas that we have shown (see p. 26) were even weaker than current behavioristic views:

[6] Compare Firth (1951*b*, p. 227 in 1957*c*): "My own approach to meaning in linguistics has always been independent of such dualisms as mind and body, language and thought, word and idea, *signifiant et signifié*, expression and content. These dichotomies are a quite unnecessary nuisance, and in my opinion should be dropped."

Every baby quickly learns the magic action of his voice, and the answering magic of his fellows. It may make him feel better, it may make him feel worse. A noise, an answering noise and 'hey presto' he either gets what he wants or what he deserves. This phonetic magic, which makes things happen and which so cogently compels people to do things, is our first and most important initiation in humanity, and the first and most fundamental language lesson we learn. That is what language really means to us — a way of doing things, of getting things done, a way of behaving and making others behave, a way of life. . . . We can only arrive at some understanding of *how* it works, if we establish with certainty that the facts of speech we are studying can be observed or regarded in actual patterns of behaviour. We must take our facts from speech sequences, verbally complete in themselves and operating in contexts of situation which are typical, recurrent, and repeatedly observable. Such contexts of situation should themselves be placed in categories of some sort, sociological and linguistic, within the wider context of culture. (p. 35)

This last comment, really, is extremely typical of Firth, and reveals clearly the reason for his almost passionate belief in the contextual theory of meaning. A few remarks selected from his popular work *Tongues of Men* are equally revealing: "Each man says more or less what the other fellow expects him to say, because in talking to the other fellow he is partly talking to himself. . . ." "Everyday conversation . . . is communal, general, and as free from unusual features of pronunciation and usage as sociability and conformity can make it. It is a sort of roughly prescribed social ritual in which you generally say what your fellows one way or the other expect you to say." "There is positive force in what you say, and there is a negative side too, because what you say shuts out most of the language of your companion, leaving him only a limited range of possible responses" (1937, pp. 93–94 in 1964). In order to set these assertions in an intellectual context, Firth indicated that his outlook accorded with that of Vilfredo Pareto, who held that ordinary language was a "derivation" — a means of justifying one's actions or attitudes (pp. 96–99). Far from acting as a mirror of the rational mind, a man's utterances reflect only the intricacies of his emotions. Firth also quoted Pareto with approval when he said that language is unable even to represent the facts of the outer world with any fidelity, that at best it is only as good as a "bad photograph which is a complete botch" (p. 100).

3. The Later Views of J. R. Firth

3.1 Introduction

From the time of his appointment to the Chair of General Linguistics until his death, Firth concerned himself mainly with the development of two new ideas, one concerning phonology and the other semantics. Both of these ideas have their foundations, to be sure, in his earlier work, but in their later developed form they have come to be considered the hallmarks of London school linguistics today. These ideas are the notions of prosodic analysis in phonology and of meaning by collocation in semantics. During this time too Firth actively supervised a considerable amount of work, especially in descriptive phonology; and beginning in 1947, papers by Firth's students and colleagues in London, and then elsewhere, began to appear, most of them concerned to apply and to extend Firth's ideas in various ways. In a fairly complete bibliography covering the period 1948–1960, G. L. Bursill-Hall has listed about one hundred such books and papers (1961, pp. 186–191). Except where these new ideas explicitly contradicted earlier ones, Firth by and large maintained intact the system of ideas that he had developed by the late 1930's. Much of Firth's later publication, in fact, constitutes a mere restatement of his earlier ideas.[1] Therefore, in discussing this

[1] For example, in connection with his concept of "context of situation," practically nothing of what he has to say in his later discussions in (1950, pp. 181–183 in 1957c) and (1957a, pp. 9–11) goes beyond what he had already said in (1935a). He remarked in (1957a, p. 9) that "no linguist has yet set up exhaustive systems of contexts of situation such that they could be considered mutually determined in

49

later period of Firth's work, we shall focus our attention primarily on these two new developments in his thinking.

3.2 Prosodic Analysis

As we have seen in Chapter 2, the goal that Firth set for phonological analysis in his early period was to list the general phonetic contexts, or syllable types, of each language, and to list the entities that substitute for one another in given positions in these syllable types and in words, which are made up of sequences of syllables. In his 1937 description of the Chinese monosyllable, he added a third goal, which was to list those phonetic features that must be considered as properties of entire syllables rather than of designated positions within them. Obviously tone in Chinese may be considered as such a feature; and similarly, he argued, the features "yotization" and "labiovelarization" may be so considered (Firth and Rogers, 1937, p. 91 in 1957c).[2]

In 1948, Firth announced a purportively new and distinctive phonological theory that took as its objective the meeting of the three goals listed. For the entities that substitute for each other in the various positions of the various syllable types he proposed the name "phonematic unit"; for the list of the syllable types, and the entities characteristic of syllables (and words) as a whole, he suggested the name "prosodic unit" (1948a, pp. 122–123 in 1957c).

In this paper Firth also explicitly rejected two of the tenets of his earlier phonological theory. First he dismissed the assumption, taken from Daniel Jones, that the upper limit on the relevant context for phonology is provided by the word:

For the purpose of distinguishing prosodic systems from phonematic systems, words will be my principal isolates. In examining these isolates, I shall not overlook the contexts from which they are taken and within which the analysis

---

function or meaning," as if this goal were readily achievable, when in fact no one as yet has shown how even a single utterance can be semantically characterized by its context of situation. Similarly, Dixon's remark in (1963, p. 48) that "theories at the interlevel of context can also be said to be at an earlier stage of development when compared to grammatical and phonological theories" misleadingly implied that the theory is developed at all. We may remark, incidentally, that Dixon has followed Malinowski and Firth in making the context of situation a convenient dumping ground for people's knowledge about the world, their own culture, etc., giving the false illusion that such facts can be systematically used in characterizing how individuals supply semantic interpretations to sentences. For a criticism of Dixon's most recent discussion of semantics, see Langendoen (forthcoming a).

[2] There the features were called "prosodic diacritica." Cf. E. Haugen's criticism of Firth's analysis, discussed on p. 44.

must be tested. Indeed, I propose to apply some of the principles of word structure to what I term "pieces" or combinations of words. (p. 122)

Phonological phenomena connected with word junction and with phrases and sentences as a whole are to be stated in prosodic terms also, Firth maintained. Second, he rejected his earlier assumption that within specific general contexts sounds are to be grouped together into one phonological entity on the basis of complementary distribution. Rather, if some of these environmentally conditioned sounds exhibit features that can be said to be characteristic of the environment in which they occur, then these features should be "abstracted out" as prosodic features of the whole context. Thus:

We are accustomed to positional criteria in classifying phonematic variants or allophones as initial, medial, intervocalic, or final. Such procedure makes abstraction of certain postulated units, *phonemes*, comprising a scatter of distributed variants (allophones). Looking at language material from a syntagmatic point of view, any phonetic feature characteristic of and peculiar to such positions or junctions can just as profitably, and perhaps more profitably, be stated as prosodies of the sentence or word. (p. 123)

Taken to its logical conclusion, *any* phonetic feature that is in any way contextually determined may be considered a prosody; or viewed in another way, prosodic analysis may be considered to be a notational convention for indicating context-sensitive phonological rules.[3] Firth himself apparently did not notice that this was the case, but others of the London school have both noticed it and sanctioned it; thus, F. R. Palmer in his discussion of palatalization in various Ethiopian Semitic languages remarked:

A statement may be made in prosodic terms, for the feature [palatalization] is prosodic in the sense that it affects the analysis of more than a single segmental unit. (1958, p. 129)

In fact, Firth and others have used the terms "prosody" and "(governed by) rule" interchangeably; and this observation, more than anything else, confirms the fact that prosodic analysis may be viewed as a notational convention for indicating phonological rules. For example, Firth listed as one of the prosodies of Egyptian Arabic "the position, nature, and quantity of the prominent" (1948, p. 130 in 1957c), and he also asserted that the position of the prominent can be predicted by rule:

[3] Where by "context" we mean "context of adjacent or nearby segments" and not that of simultaneously occurring features.

In the . . . [Egyptian Arabic] words the prominent is marked by an accent. This is, however, not necessary, since prominence can be stated in rules without exception, given the . . . analysis of syllabic structure. (p. 129)

As Firth formulated it, and as it has been generally practiced within the London school, prosodic analysis (following standard practice, we shall use the term "prosodic analysis" to mean Firth's phonological theory involving analysis of phonetic features into prosodic and phonematic units) has followed the following two principles: (1) no assumptions are made concerning phonological universals, features are assigned to prosodic or phonematic units *ad hoc*, depending upon the language; and (2) the analysis involves nothing more than a classification of phonetic data to these systems. The following hypothetical analysis illustrates what we may consider orthodox London school principles.

Let L be a language in which the vowel of the penultimate syllable is long when it precedes a voiced consonant, and otherwise either long or short. In this language, we may associate with word-final position (or, alternatively, with the position occupied by the consonant following the vowel of the penultimate syllable) a prosody having two "terms," v and $ṽ$. Associated with v are the phonetic features (1) voicing of the consonant following the penultimate vowel, and (2) length of the penultimate vowel. Associated with $ṽ$ is simply voicelessness of the consonant following the penultimate vowel. Occupying the phonematic position corresponding to the vowel of the penultimate syllable is a unit that is not designated for length in case the prosodic term v occurs in the word (since the length of that vowel is associated with the prosody). The following consonant is also not designated for voicing, since voicing is a property of the prosody consisting of the terms v and $ṽ$, and by hypothesis all words are "marked" as having this prosody.

The context-sensitive rule corresponding to this prosodic statement is simply[4]

[4] This rule may be read as follows: any segment that is specified as being both vocalic and nonconsonantal is further specified as being long when it precedes a voiced consonant, which is followed by zero or more segments that are either consonantal or nonvocalic, a vocalic and nonconsonantal segment, zero or more segments that are either consonantal or nonvocalic, and a word-boundary. The symbol V is used as a "cover" symbol for true vowels (segments that are both vocalic and nonconsonantal), and C for anything that is not a V (thus either a true consonant, liquid, or glide). Throughout this study, rules will be given in terms of phonological features, and we shall generally follow the usage of R. Jakobson and M. Halle (1956). An integer subscript on a cover symbol or segment means that at least as many segments having the features designated as is indicated by the integer must occur in that position; thus C_1 means one or more nonvowels. An integer superscript means that that many segments at most may occur in the designated

$$\begin{bmatrix} +\text{voc} \\ -\text{cns} \end{bmatrix} \rightarrow [+\text{lng}] \Big/ - \begin{bmatrix} +\text{voi} \\ +\text{cns} \end{bmatrix} C_o V C_o \ \#$$

It will be noted that in our proposed prosodic analysis both the feature specified as a consequence of the rule and certain features of the environment were indiscriminately lumped together as "exponents" of the prosody. This, as we shall show in the next chapter, is a general characteristic of prosodic descriptions. It is generally left up to the ingenuity of the interpreter to determine, from a given prosodic statement, what is the set of rule-governed features and what is the set of conditioning features; this is especially so in the case of the work of such practitioners as R. K. Sprigg, and to some extent W. S. Allen, who insist that prosodic analysis is an *alternative* to an analysis which states rules rather than simply a notational restatement of such an analysis.[5]

Elements that are given phonematic status in a prosodic analysis consist of those phonetic features whose occurrence is not context dependent, or, to be more precise, whose occurrence is not governed by constraints found outside the segment that they occupy. As far as I know, only W. S. Allen has raised the theoretical question of whether features whose occurrence depends on simultaneously occurring fea-

---

position; thus C^1 means at most one nonvowel. Therefore the symbol C_1^1 means exactly one nonvowel.

We may give as hypothetical words in language L the following: [pata], [pa:ta], and [pa:da]. The form *[pada] is of course excluded. The prosodic formulas for the three words may be written $paTa^\gamma$, $pa:Ta^\gamma$, and $paTa^\gamma$, where T means an alveolar (say) plosive that is not specified for voicing, and A symbolizes an open vowel that is not specified for length.

[5] Allen's position will be discussed further in Chapter 4, section 3. Since Sprigg's work will not be discussed in Chapter 4, we shall give a characteristic statement here to illustrate his position. "A [nother] advantage of prosodic analysis is that it enables one to avoid the concept of assimilation. . . . There is a further obstacle in the way of applying the assimilation concept to the vowel-harmony material presented in this article. This concept would seem to require an assimilator and an assimilee. Thus, the vowel ɛ of the assimilee Syllable *thɛmba* 'he smoked', would be said to have been replaced by the vowel *i* under the influence of the vowel *i* of the following assimilator Syllable *gi*. In this example the assimilation relationship is of the type assimilee-assimilator. In, for example, *simbe:* 'did you catch', on the other hand, the relationship is of the type assimilator-assimilee: the vowel ɛ of the assimilee Syllable *be:* would be said to have been replaced by the vowel *e* under the influence of the vowel *i* of the preceding assimilator Syllable *sin*. Difficulties arise when both Syllables of the assimilation are of the same type: assimilee-assimilee, e.g. *de:b:ɛ* 'did you stay'; or assimilator-assimilator, e.g. *simgi-*, 'he will catch'. Where both Syllables are assimilators, which is assimilated to which?" (1951, p. 137)

tures should be considered prosodic (that is, predictable by rule). In his paper, "Aspiration in the Hāṛautī Nominal," he remarked:

It will have been noted that the phonological statement here proposed specifies [voice] as one of the exponents of phonematic units symbolized *r, l, n, m, ṛ, ḷ, ṇ, w̃, v, y*, or as a coarticulatory exponent of a prosodic unit referred to their place (and similarly [voicelessness] as an exponent of units symbolized *s*). It might be objected, particularly by proponents of the 'distinctive-feature' technique, that certain other coarticulated data allotted to such units (e.g., nasality, laterality, flap; friction) invariably imply voice (or voicelessness); and hence that, these other data having been described in the statement of exponents, the inclusion of [voice] or [voicelessness] is 'redundant'. (1957, p. 85)

If we agree that Allen's notational decisions embody assertions about the validity of methods for representing the phonological structure of language, he is then making the assertion that context-free phonological rules, say of the type

$$[+\text{nsl}] \rightarrow [+\text{voi}],$$

are not allowed in linguistic description, whereas context-sensitive rules are allowed. Clearly this contention is formally unmotivated; no reason of a formal nature can be given to exclude automatically context-free phonological rules but permit context-sensitive ones, and furthermore the contention results in a much less adequate description, since obvious generalizations about language are being missed. It is true that Allen did go on to say that an alternative prosodic formulation is possible which incorporates a "general statement . . . regarding this implication, thus avoiding the necessity for specifying [voice] or [voicelessness] on each occasion" (p. 85), but he did not consider the issue a serious enough one to indicate what this reformulation would look like.

It should be apparent from this discussion that, aside from certain small differences, Firth's prosodic analysis is identical with what has come to be known in America as "long-component" analysis, where we consider long components to be the counterpart to prosodies and the features that remain upon extraction of the long components to correspond to phonematic units. It will be noted that the objectives of long-component analysis are very similar to the objectives of prosodic analysis, namely, to provide a notation in which context-sensitive features are segregated from context-independent ones, where, roughly speaking, the former are written over or under the line, and the latter are written on the line. Harris, in 1944, stated the objective as follows:

In our second operation we consider the usual type of limitation of distribution, in which a phoneme that occurs in most environments is limited by never appearing in certain positions. Here no solution is possible within the methods of segmental phonemics. The difficulty with the archiphoneme device, and with the statements about distribution relations between phonemes, is that they seek only to find a relation or common factor among the phonemes that can or cannot occur in a given environment. But there also exists a relation between the phonemes which occur in a given environment and the environment itself, namely the fact that they occur next to each other. That relation exists, for instance, between English /ŋ/ and /k/, but not between /ŋ/ and /t/. If we are willing to break phonemes up into simultaneous components, we restate relation as a factor common to /ŋ/ and /k/ but not to /t/; and we say that /ŋ/ and /k/ each contain a certain component (say, back position) and that this component spreads over the length of two phonemes when the first is nasal. . . . By the use of components which are defined so as to extend over a number of phoneme places, we thus circumvent the limitation in distribution of the phonemes. This is not merely a trick, concealing the limitations of the phonemes in the definitions of the components. For the components are generalized phonemes: they appear concurrently with each other as well as next to each other, and they may have a length of several phoneme-places as well as of one phoneme-place. (1944, p. 130 in Joos, 1957)

The objective is similarly defined in Harris' book *Structural Linguistics* (Chapter 10).

The nearly complete identity of the objectives of prosodic analysis and long-component analysis cannot be stressed too strongly, in view of the fact that members of the London school have long made it a point to assert the superiority of their phonological theory to contemporary neo-Bloomfieldian phonological theory. It turns out, however, that their criticisms have almost always been directed at strictly segmental phonology and distributional analysis — precisely those aspects of neo-Bloomfieldian phonological theory that Harris criticized just as effectively back in 1944. Again, only Allen has attempted a criticism of long-component analysis from the point of view of prosodic analysis;[6] this fact alone makes Allen's paper "Aspiration in the Hāṛautī Nominal," in which the criticism appears, perhaps the most important single paper from a theoretical point of view to come out of the London school. Allen first criticizes Harris' long-component analysis because it identifies long-component features (context-dependent ones) with segmental features that are not context-dependent, when they are, in fact, the same feature:

[6] Firth made an oblique reference to Harris' long components by criticizing a comparison of his own techniques with those of Harris that had been made by C. C. Fries and K. L. Pike, in Firth and Adam (1950, p. 173 in 1957c).

The term [domain] has previously been used by Z. Harris in his discussion of "phonemic long components" (*Methods in Structural Linguistics*, pp. 125 ff.), which contains certain suggestions tending towards a prosodic approach; Harris's method is, however, entirely unprosodic in its phonemic presuppositions, which lead to such pseudo-problems as that admitted on p. 132, n. 7: "One of the major difficulties in deciding whether to extract a component is the requirement that if we extract a component from the sequence /XY/ by saying that it equals /$\overline{\text{WU}}$/, we must extract it from /X/ and from /Y/ even when they are not in the sequence." (1957, p. 71)

It is difficult to see why Harris should have been criticized for this convention; if carried through consistently, it provides for an analysis of each segmental phonological unit of a language into those features that are also relevant to statements of context dependencies (cf. Harris, 1951, pp. 147–149), and this is certainly a commendable goal, since it enables one to state generalizations of the type missed by Allen (see p. 54). It may be noted, further, that prosodies have been defined by R. M. W. Dixon in such a way that they are precisely the same thing as Harris' long components: "Prosodies need not be delimited in statement, that is either their beginning or their end or both need not be explicitly noted; they can be associated with any extent of phonological 'text' (the minimum extent being a single phoneme)" (1963, p. 43).

Allen also criticizes the approach for starting from a phonemic analysis rather than relating directly to the phonetic level. But since Harris' phonemic analysis stands at least theoretically in a biunique relationship with the phonetic level, the only possible consequence of starting from the phonemic rather than the phonetic level is that certain allophonic features will not turn up as long components, whereas they may turn up as prosodies in a prosodic analysis. Since in any event the features will be the same, the difference is purely notational.

One further theoretical issue raised in Allen's paper requires comment; that is, whether a "simultaneous allotment of any given phonic data to both phonematic and prosodic units" should be permitted (1957, p. 69). Allen suggested as a natural convention that it should not be permitted, whereas Firth maintained that it should:

It is . . . quite likely that certain phonic details may be included in the phonetic characteristics of prosodic elements and structures as well as in those of phonematic units and systems. There are, so to speak, two distinct 'syndromes' and there is no tautology or falsification if there is some overlap in 'symptoms.' (1957a, p. 15)

We can illustrate this issue easily by means of our hypothetical analysis of language *L* (see pp. 52–53); in fact, our analysis embodies Allen's convention, which says, for instance, that vowels in the context

$$-\begin{bmatrix} +\text{voi} \\ +\text{cns} \end{bmatrix} C_o V C_o \; \#$$

are not phonematically indicated for length. Firth's convention permits that vowel to be phonematically long, so the application of the rule given on page 53 may be vacuous. Thus the issue comes down to whether or not the rules embodied in the prosodies may have vacuous application or not.

Because of the classificatory nature of prosodic analysis (that is, it permits only the "allotment" of phonetic data to phonological systems), it prohibits the specification of penultimate vowels preceding voiced consonants in language L to be phonematically specified as short. As a consequence of this restriction (common to both prosodic analysis and long-component analysis), the rule on page 53 is not permitted to *change* the underlying feature specification of the affected vowel. To see what effects this restriction entails, let us suppose that in language L monosyllabic suffixes may be added to stems (which may also function independently as full words). In particular, let [tak] be such an affix, which when added to [pa:ta] yields the form [pa:tatak], when added to [pata] yields [patatak], but when added to [pa:da] yields either [pa:datak] or [padatak], with two different meanings corresponding to two different meanings associated with the form [pa:da]. A natural solution in long-component terms is to say that /p$\overline{\text{ata}}$/ [pa:da] (where the superscript bar is the long component corresponding to the prosody *v*) represents two homophonous morphemes, one of which has the morphophonemic alternant /pa:da/ when it occurs before /-tak/, and the other the alternant /pada/ when it occurs before /-tak/. However, since the London school has rejected the morphophonemic level, this recourse is not open to them. They are obliged to say that the forms [pa:datak] and [padatak], which would presumably be written *pa:daTak*$^{\bar{v}}$ and *padaTak*$^{\bar{v}}$, respectively (see fn. 4), are completely unrelated to the form [pa:da], which would be transcribed *pATa*^{v}, or if Firth's convention is adopted, *pa:Ta*^{v}, *pAda*^{v}, or *pa:da*^{v}, depending upon the whim of the analyst. It is one of the most curious facts about Firth's position that he took pride in being obliged to consider such forms unrelated:

It is unnecessary, indeed perhaps inadvisable, to attempt a structural and systemic account of a language as a whole. Any given or selected restricted language . . . is, from the present point of view multistructural and poly-systemic. (p. 30)

If, on the contrary, we permit rules to change underlying feature specifications, in particular if we allow the rule on page 53 to apply to vowels distinctively indicated as being either long or short, and then if we write the two morphemes that are both pronounced [pa:da] as *pa:da* and *pada*, respectively, the rule automatically accounts correctly for the pronunciation of all the forms that we have cited, without recourse to any additional morphophonemic statements or to the suggestion that obviously related forms are phonologically unrelated. Similarly, if language *L* also contained a suffix [dak], this rule would correctly account for the forms [pa:da:dak] (corresponding to [pa:datak]) and [pada:dak] (corresponding to [padatak]), whereas an additional morphophonemic statement would be required in the long-component analysis and a third unrelated system would have to be supposed in the prosodic analysis.

London school analysts have advanced one other argument in support of their contention that prosodic analysis is superior to any contemporary American phonological theory based on segmental phonemics. They suggest that since prosodic analysis permits the statement of grammatical environments as part of the prosodies (or as part of their domain), any phonological phenomenon that is conditioned on the basis of grammatical categorization and the like can be handled directly in a prosodic description, whereas in a phonemic description, which insists on segregating the phonological facts from the grammatical ones, it cannot be handled directly. This argument has been most clearly formulated by R. H. Robins in his "Vowel Nasality in Sundanese: A Phonological and Grammatical Study" (1957). Robins maintained:

. . . the feature of vowel nasality could be treated phonemically, and the same phonetic observations accounted for. (p. 95)

But any phonemic analysis would be obliged to treat vowel nasality as phonemic, because it is partially grammatically conditioned and such nearly minimal pairs as [mãrios] and [mãriãk] may be attested. The nasalization of the second vowel in [mãriãk] can, however, be predicted once one knows the grammatical composition of the word. Robins concludes from this that the prosodic analysis which he proposes is superior to a phonemic analysis because he predicts all instances of vowel nasalization directly. Robins' argument succeeds, however, only against a phonological theory which maintains that the one permitted phonological representation is the phonemic one. American phonologists, however, have generally maintained that a morphophonemic level of representation is also required; and there would be no difficulty in predicting phonemic vowel nasality in Sundanese on the morphophonemic level. To show that his analysis is superior to a phonemic and a morphophonemic analysis, in which morphophonemic vowel nasality is predictable, Robins is required to show that the introduction of a phonemic level results in a complication of the statement of the phonological rules embodied in his description. This he does not do, and it can in fact be shown that there is a phonemic solution for which it cannot be done.[7]

In a recent article, furthermore, Robins has made the suggestion that a prosodic analysis may be supplemented by a phonemic analysis for the purposes of providing a "reading transcription," presumably at no extra cost. He remarked, in connection with E. J. A. Henderson's description of Siamese (1949):

This article also shows the very different end result of a prosodic analysis as contrasted with a phonemic transcription. The prosodic analysis of a text or stretch of utterance can be diagrammed, but not transcribed. The diagram can be interpreted and reveals the syntagmatic, structural relationships of the elements involved; it does not produce a 'reading transcription', for which a phonemic type of procedure will always be necessary. (Robins, 1963, pp. 31–32)

Much the same point has been made by Palmer (1958a).

The question that immediately arises is what are the necessary conditions for the prosodic "diagram"? On this question Firth had little to say beyond remarking that the diagram must not be unidimensional (1948, p. 138 in 1957c). The convention usually adopted is that for

---

[7] This is to say that Robins in particular and the London school in general has failed so far to come up with an example that has the property that when a phonemic analysis is introduced between the London school "level" of analysis and the phonetic level, the over-all description is necessarily complicated. So far, they have given no cases parallel to the one described by Morris Halle for Russian, in which he showed that the introduction of a phonemic level between his level of phonology (which may be called "systematic phonemics") and phonetics necessarily complicates the description (cf. Halle, 1959, pp. 22–23).

Despite this failure, Robins' article is to be commended for its place in the assault on the position of no "levels mixing" between phonology and syntax. Robins' position is that morpheme class identification is required in phonological descriptions, placing it in the third position in the hierarchy of increasing freedom to mix levels. The first position, usually identified with C. F. Hockett, B. Bloch, and others, countenances strict separation of levels, while the second position, associated with K. L. Pike, allows morpheme boundaries identification to play a phonological role. The fourth position, that of generative phonologists generally, is that the entire surface phrase marker has phonological significance.

each prosody a position in the phonematic sequence is designated (called its "focus") and also its extent of realization over the sequence (called its "domain"). However, a consistent use of notational conventions has not been adopted within the London school; and there are instances in the literature of spurious notational simplifications being paraded as genuine economy of description. Perhaps the most notable instance of this is provided by A. E. Sharp in his discussion of tone in disyllabic nouns in the Chaga language of East Africa (1954). After showing that disyllabic nouns may be categorized into nine tonal classes, Sharp proposed as a phonological analysis that each disyllabic noun of the language be labeled with an integer from one to nine, depending upon which tone class it belongs to. He then proclaimed the superiority of his analysis over any possible "tonemic" one, precisely because the tonemic statement would have to indicate a great deal of tonal sandhi whereas his solution is elegantly simple, requiring only nine invariant symbols!

Despite the fact that London school phonologists have been quite articulate in their criticisms of other phonological approaches, they have had little to say concerning the criteria for evaluating phonological descriptions, in particular their own. Firth has proposed a general condition for linguistic descriptions, in particular phonological descriptions, that they "renew connection" with phonetic and situational facts, but it is not clear what is meant by this condition. R. K. Sprigg's interpretation, for phonology, was simply that the description should ensure that it is related to reality. Thus,

Since all abstractions at the phonological level, whether prosodic or phonematic, are stated through the medium of *ad hoc* systems, and the value of each term in a system is in proportion to the total number of terms in that system; it is clear that phonological symbols are purely formulaic, and in themselves without precise articulatory implications. In order therefore to secure 'renewal of connection' with utterances, it becomes necessary to cite abstractions at another level of analysis, the Phonetic level: abstractions at the Phonetic level are stated as criteria for setting up the phonological categories concerned, and as exponents of phonological categories and terms. (1957, p. 107)[8]

[8] Sprigg's remark that the number of elements that may substitute for one another solely defines their value is characteristic of the "numerology" of the London school. Compare Firth's definition of "grammatical meaning" in (1957a, p. 22): ". . . grammatical 'meanings' are determined by their inter-relations in the systems set up for that language. 'A nominative in a four case system would in this sense necessarily have a different "meaning" from a nominative in a two case or fourteen case system, for example.' "

Similarly, R. H. Robins (1963, p. 20): "Each system set up for a particular structural place is peculiar to that place, and the commuting terms in it are not necessarily

Another interpretation has been given by Robins, namely, that the phonological analysis established on the basis of a finite corpus should also prove adequate to handle data not used in the establishment of the analysis:

In spoken utterance, sounds and the attributes of sounds are the exponents of elements of structures. The converse relation to exponency is 'renewal of connection', by which analyses are tested and justified. When structures and systems have been set up for a language, or some definable part of a language, on the basis of a limited body of material with the assumption that this is a typical sample, the analysis is tested and used in application to further material of the same sort and from the same language, and if exponents can be found for the elements of the structure that has been posited, the analysis is said to renew connection with the language. (1963, p. 21)

But even under Robins' definition of "renewal of connection," London school phonologists have generally claimed the right to declare in advance that they will only consider a restricted part of a language in their description and that linguistic evidence from outside this "language under description" has absolutely no bearing on this description, even though that evidence is from the same language. A typical expression of this "right" has been made by Palmer:

It is not required that the exponents of gemination shall be the same for all types of plural, or that the differences shall be accounted for by a phonological 'explanation', and, still less, that the phonological analysis shall be integrated with the analysis of other, unrelated data [of the same language]. (1957, p. 147)

The point of view that will be insisted upon here, in contrast to this, is that all linguistic data in a particular language are relevant to each other. This position, moreover, is not incompatible with the observation that the vocabulary of a particular language may have different sources, each with a different "phonology" (cf. Firth, 1948a, p. 121).

3.3 Meaning by Collocation

Throughout this later period Firth maintained intact his understanding of the notion of "meaning" as first expressed comprehensively in "Technique of Semantics." He devoted his paper "Modes of Meaning" (1951a, pp. 190–215 in 1957c) to going over approximately the

---

to be identified with those operative in a system at a different place. Where the number of commuting terms is different, the systems are different, and each term is different from its apparent counterpart elsewhere, because of the different paradigmatic relations necessarily holding between the terms of numerically different systems,"

same ground. In this later paper, however, one of the five dimensions of meaning, the lexical dimension (or mode), received much greater attention, and the meaning that was supposedly contributed by this mode was also given a new name, "meaning by collocation" (p. 144). The following extended citation will give an accurate picture of what Firth had in mind concerning this notion:

This kind of study of the distribution of common words may be classified into general or usual collocations and more restricted technical or personal collocations. The commonest sentences in which the words *horse, cow, pig, swine, dog* are used with adjectives in nominal phrases, and also with verbs in the simple present, indicate characteristic distributions in collocability which may be regarded as a label of meaning in describing the English of any particular social group or indeed of one person. The word 'time' can be used in collocations with or without articles, determinatives, or pronouns. And it can be collocated with *saved, spent, wasted, frittered away*, with *presses, flies*, and with a variety of particles, even with *no*. Just as phonetic, phonological, and grammatical forms well established and habitual in any close social group provide a basis for the mutual expectancies of words and sentences at those levels, and also the sharing of these common features, so also the study of the usual collocations of a particular literary form or genre or of a particular author makes possible a clearly defined and precisely stated contribution to what I have termed the spectrum of descriptive linguistics, which handles and states meaning by dispersing it in a range of techniques working at a series of levels. . . . Meaning by collocation is an abstraction at the syntagmatic level and is not directly concerned with the conceptual or idea approach to the meaning of words. One of the meanings of *night* is its collocability with *dark*, and of *dark*, of course, collocation with *night*. (pp. 195–196)

Elsewhere, Firth maintained that if part of the meaning of a word is given by its possible collocations, this is the same as saying that "the meaning of words lies in their use" (1957*a*, p. 11). Firth took these words from Wittgenstein (1953, p. 80), indicating that he understood Wittgenstein to say that the meaning of words is given by their strictly linguistic context.

Firth's proposals for studying words in lexical contexts amount, however, not to assertions about semantics but about stylistics, and even as such they are not particularly suggestive ones. They fail to distinguish, for example, stylistically neutral expressions, or clichés, from genuine idioms, since they both meet the condition that they should consist of words appearing in habitual collocation in the speech or writing of a given individual or social group. The distinction between them, however, is a crucial one for both stylistics and semantics; for stylistics, because presumably a person can make effective use of an idiom but not of a cliché (except perhaps in a pun), and for semantics, because idioms must be considered as being themselves lexical items (although they are composed of smaller ones) whereas the meaning of clichés is given by composition from the meanings of their component lexical items (cf. Katz and Fodor, 1963).

The fact that Firth's proposals concerning collocation are proposals about stylistics rather than semantics has been recognized and admitted by members of the London school. Thus Robins has said:

> It may be surmised that part of what is loosely and generally called style in literature depends on the skilful exploitation and variation of possible and habitual collocations in the language employed. A good deal of Firth's 'Modes of Meaning' is concerned with the stylistic analysis, in terms of collocations, of two very different examples of literary English. (1963, p. 24)

W. Haas, on the other hand, has suggested that the notion of meaning by collocation of a lexical item be interpreted as the distributional properties of that item in the sentences of the language of which it is a part:

> Both, form and meaning, are obtained by the same method of substitution: the form of a sign by substituting *in* it, the meaning by substituting *for* it . . . substitutions for *cat*, in more comprehensive units such as *The ——— caught the mouse, I bought fish for my ———,* etc., display its meaning; its privilege of occurring in those contexts with a certain distribution of frequencies among the occurrences, *is* the linguistic meaning of *cat*. The distinctive elements of *cat* are its form; its being itself a distinctive element is its meaning. (1954, p. 80)

The impossibility of characterizing the meaning of lexical items by their distributional properties can, however, be shown through a slight modification of an argument used by Y. Bar-Hillel to prove the impossibility of morpheme *identification* by distributional means (1954, p. 233). If Haas intends us to take as the set of defining contexts the totality of all possible sentences of a language such as English, then the distribution of such morphemes as *green* and *red* "within this totality is *almost* exactly the same, i.e. the same up to a subset of special environments which will cause trouble to any consistent and would-be simple description" (p. 233). Their "distribution of frequencies among the occurrences" will also be identical; each occurrence will be associated with a frequency that is indistinguishable from zero. If, on the other hand, Haas intends us to take as the defining contexts the totality of sentences that have been uttered up to a particular point, say the present, then each new utterance changes the meaning of one or more lexical items of the language; and to effect a really drastic change in meaning, all one has to do is to utter the same sentence repeatedly for a long period of time.

Any formulation that, like Firth's or Haas's, attempts to assign meaning to lexical items on the basis of their occurrence in utterances, is actually approaching the problem of semantic description backwards. Consider Firth's example of *dark night*. Firth was in effect arguing that given this phrase, with some determinate meaning, we can then say something about the meaning of each word. The goal of semantics should be, rather, to show how the meaning of such phrases as *dark night* is determinable from a knowledge of the meaning of the lexical items comprising them and the syntactic relationships that are found in them. Once this goal is set, then the question of the optimal method for representing the meaning of lexical items can be raised (cf. Katz and Fodor, 1963). With this approach to semantics, one is able to speak of general rules which amalgamate the meaning of nouns and adjectives to yield the meaning of noun phrases, of verbs and their complements to yield the meaning of verb phrases, and of subjects and predicates to yield the meaning of sentences. Any attempt to determine the meaning of lexical items by collocation in phrases cannot take advantage of the regularities of the language, such as the grammatical composition of noun phrases, but is obliged to state meanings *ad hoc* for each collocation.

Firth's proposals for dictionary making are of interest in relation to his concern with meaning by collocation. Firth suggested the following procedures for lexicography: first collect "exhaustive collocations of the selected words," and then proceed as follows:

> It will . . . be found that meaning by collocation will suggest grouping of the collocations into a manageable number of sets.
>
> Each set of grouped collocations may suggest an arbitrary definition of the word, compound or phrase which is being studied in collocation.
>
> If the materials are being collected from informants, *definition texts may be recorded* [emphasis mine] by them in their own language, as their own version of the meanings, group by group. Definition texts provided in this way can be extremely informative, but must be critically handled.
>
> Draft entries can now be made, one for each group, definitions can be given and from the *collocations* one or two may be chosen to become *citations* keyed to the definitions. (1957a, p. 26)

For Firth to say that certain collocations have greater semantic significance than others and deserve the status of "definition texts" certainly begs the question, if meaning by collocation depends solely on the study of actual occurrence in collocation. His belief that certain collocations are more significant than others betrays, in fact, his covert presupposition that lexical items have inherent meanings, of which definition texts are simply paraphrases.

3.4 Views on Syntax

During this later period of Firth's work, neither he nor his colleagues in the London school made any substantive theoretical contribution to the study of syntax or morphology, and as we have already remarked (see p. 49 and fn. 1), practically no further work was done to refine the notion "context of situation." Only an article by T. F. Mitchell (1957) can be cited as an attempt to describe the meanings of words in terms of context of situation, but upon examination of this paper it will be seen that it properly belongs to the realm of ethnography and not of semantics.

In syntax, P. Postal has shown that the grammatical theory of M. A. K. Halliday amounts to a slot-and-filler variety of phrase structure description (1964, pp. 97 ff.), and the same can be said of the somewhat earlier theoretical proposals by Robins (1953).[9] It would seem that Firth himself held, if anything, a weaker view of syntax, namely that it is finite state. The only means by which we can evaluate Firth's view of syntax is by studying the terminological suggestions he made, since he published no syntactic descriptions during his lifetime.

The most important term that Firth proposed for the study of syntax is colligation; in his "Synopsis of Linguistic Theory," he introduced the term as follows:

The statement of meaning at the grammatical level is in terms of word and sentence classes or of similar categories and of the inter-relation of those categories in colligations. Grammatical relations should not be regarded as relations, between words as such — between 'watched' and 'him' in 'I watched him' — but between a personal pronoun, first person singular nominative, the past tense of a transitive verb and the third person pronoun singular in the oblique or objective form. (1957a, p. 13)

Thus, Firth defined the notion "colligation" as playing the same role in syntax as "collocation" plays in lexicography, despite his later claim that "a colligation is not to be interpreted as abstraction in parallel with a collocation of exemplifying words in a text" (p. 14). The reason for this latter assertion is that he considered elements in colligation to be discontinuous. But it turns out that Firth's proposals

---

[9] Cf. his diagrams, pp. 122–123, which show that he was working with a phrase structure hierarchy consisting of sentences made up of clauses, clauses of phrases, and phrases of words.

for handling discontinuous constituents do not do real violence to the parallel between collocation and colligation; these proposals amount to a consideration of discontinuous constituents, such as concord elements, as the grammatical analogues of prosodies:

The various structures of sentences in any given language, comprising for example at least two nominal pieces and a verbal piece must be collated, and such categories as voice, mood, affirmative, negative, tense, aspect, gender, number, person and case, if found applicable and valid in descriptive statement, are to be abstracted from, and referred back to the sentence as a whole. The exponents of the categories may be cumulate or discontinuous or both, and their phonetic description may necessitate the use of terms and notation not based on orthography or, indeed, on any scheme of segmental letters in the tradition of the roman alphabet. (p. 20)

Viewed in this way, discontinuous constituents can be considered as exponents of "sentential long components" imposed on a linear, Markovian array of grammatical categories. The notion "colligation" was also used by M. A. K. Halliday, in his dissertation *The Language of the Chinese "Secret History of the Mongols"* (1959), in a characteristically *ad hoc* manner to define such entities as "sentence." After defining "piece" as that part of the text occurring between two punctuation marks, he continued:

The sentence that is set up must be (as a category) larger than the piece, since certain forms which are final to the piece are not final to the sentence. Of the relation between the two we may say so far that: 1, a piece ending in liau or je will normally be final in the sentence; 2, a piece ending in ši₂, ŋa, heu or saŋgeu₂ will normally be non-final in a sentence; 3, a piece ending in lai or kiu may be either final or non-final in a sentence. (p. 46)

The futility of attempts to provide definitions in terms of superficial formal characteristics, such as word occurrence in connection with punctuation marks, should be apparent.

In "Synopsis" Firth also discussed two other technical terms for syntax, *order* and *sequence*, which he related in the following way:

The statement of the colligation of a grammatical category deals with a *mutually expectant order* of categories, attention being focussed on one category at a time. If two or more categories are in the focus of attention, the study of their colligations is in similar mutually expectant orders. Such categories are not considered as having *positions* in *sequence*, but can be said to be placed in order. (1957a, p. 17)

It is not clear what Firth meant by this statement; possibly order can be interpreted as the relationship between linearly colligated grammatical categories and the sentential long components, and sequence can be interpreted as the physical linear order of sentences as they are spoken or written. In "Structure and System in the Abaza Verbal Complex," Allen gives a different and much deeper interpretation of the distinction; for a discussion of his use of the terms, see Chapter 4, section 5.

In morphology, the London school has produced at least two important descriptive works, one by R. H. Robins on Sundanese (1959), and the other by F. R. Palmer on Tigre (1962), but both of these works are strictly within the item-and-arrangement descriptive framework already well established in American morphological descriptions.

3.5 Rejection of Universal Grammar

Firth and his colleagues have explicitly rejected the validity of universal grammar, and indeed of universal phonology; one of Firth's strongest criticisms of Malinowski applied to the latter's assumptions concerning universal grammar (1957*b*, p. 109). In phonology, Firth stated that the phonematic and prosodic units should be "systematically stated *ad hoc* for each language" (1948, p. 131 in 1957*c*); yet, as A. A. Hill has pointed out, it seemed that the more that could be described prosodically, the better Firth would like it (1961, p. 468). Sounds that could be expected to be involved as exponents of prosodies included liquids, nasals, semivowels, the Semitic laryngeals, the glottal stop, schwa, and *h* (1948, p. 131 in 1957*c*). A remark which reveals that Firth really had a universalist bias is the following:

Such common phenomena as elision, liaison, anaptyxis, the use of so-called 'cushion' consonants or 'sounds for euphony' are involved in this study of prosodies. (p. 131)[10]

[10] Upon examination of the illustrations and fragments of prosodic analysis applied to such languages as Arabic, Hindi, and English in "Sounds and Prosodies," one quickly realizes that Firth's assignment of features to prosodies and phonematic units is not at all *ad hoc*. Firth was particularly concerned in this paper to show how pharyngeal and laryngeal sounds tend to distribute themselves over syllables through time (so that the pharyngeals are phonematic in classical Arabic but prosodies in the modern dialects) or through space (so that *h* is phonematic in Eastern Hindustani but prosodic in Western Hindustani, while in Panjabi it comes out as a tonal phenomenon). Thus my attempt to indicate the interconvertability of prosodic and long-component analysis is to show only that given an analysis in one system one can come up with an equivalent in the other, not that the kinds of phonological problems tackled by followers of the two systems were similar. Another way to state the difference between Harris and Firth is to say that the former was attempting to develop a redundancy-free phonological notation, while the latter was seeking a notation that would highlight the relationship between phonetic detail and context of occurrence.

Firth's argument that phonological systems must be stated *ad hoc* for each language appears to consist of two points: (1) that the phonological features necessary to categorize particular phonematic or prosodic units may differ from the set of features which are needed to categorize other phonematic or prosodic units either in the same language or in different languages, and (2) the particular phonetic exponents associated with a particular phonematic or prosodic unit may differ. The first point, however, is a truism, and if the phonological features themselves are taken to be universals, it has no bearing on the question of universal phonological categories. Similarly, the second point has no real bearing on the question. Consider, for example, a language with a particular phonological feature: when this is associated with bilabial or alveolar plosives it is realized as voiced implosion (that is [ɓ] and [ɗ]), when associated with the velar plosive it is realized as voiceless glottalization [k'], and when associated with the alveolar sibilant it is realized as voiceless affrication [ts]. A feature having these characteristics has been described by J. Carnochan in his discussion of Hausa, and he chose to call it "glottalization" (1952, p. 93). It is perhaps true that there is no other language in the world in which a feature that may be called glottalization has these particular phonetic realizations, yet this does not mean that we cannot identify glottalization as a universal phonological feature. It simply means that the rules for implementing the pronunciation of elements classified with the same feature in two different languages may be different, a point made quite obvious by Sapir in his "Sound Patterns in Language" (1925).

Firth's arguments against syntactic universals fail for about the same reasons. His major argument seems to have been simply that since the meaning of grammatical categories differs from one language to another, no substantive identification of the categories is permissible. But since he never provided any clear account of what grammatical meaning *is*, it is difficult to take this argument very seriously. The following citation is typical of the statements that Firth made on the subject of "grammatical meaning":

The present writer illustrates what is termed 'grammatical meaning' by concocting such sentences as 'My doctor's great grandfather will be singeing the cat's wings', or 'She slowly rushed upstairs to the cellar and turned the kettle out to boil two fires.' (1957a, p. 8)

Firth was, however, unwilling to accept the logical consequences of the denial of universal grammar, namely, the complete abandonment of the conceptual and terminological tradition of grammar, which had been built up over the preceding two millennia:

Every analysis of a particular 'language' must of necessity determine the values of *ad hoc* categories to which traditional names are given. (p. 21)

But then the question arises: Which names go with which categories? There are only two possibilities: (1) they are assigned at random, or (2) they are assigned on the basis of universal grammar. It is doubtful that Firth would seriously have maintained the former, so that by refusing to give up the traditional names he in fact failed to renounce universal grammar. This same argument holds for Halliday's putative rejection of universal grammar:

The 'structural' linguist, while attempting to develop descriptive methods that are general . . . will be unwilling to claim universality for any formally established category; since, while, for example, it may be convenient in the description of all languages so far studied to give the name 'verb' to one class of one unit, this is not a universal statement: the 'verb' is redefined in the description of each language. (1957, p. 57)

Robins, however, has admitted that the substantive identification of the categories "noun" and "verb" in different languages is more than a terminological convenience, and the argument he gave to prove this point is precisely part of an argument for believing that they are in fact universal grammatical categories:

. . . grammatical analysis in terms of a basic distinction of nominal and verbal categories succeeds in new fields and stands critical examination in the older areas of language study where so much else of traditional grammar has had to be abandoned. (1952, p. 296)

Appendix. The Views of J. Lyons in *Structural Semantics*

In this section we examine the views on syntax and semantics expressed by John Lyons in his *Structural Semantics*. As was noted in the introduction, this work was completed essentially in 1961, and was written under the supervision of W. S. Allen and R. H. Robins. Lyons develops an eclectic theory, drawing not only on principles of the London school but also on certain traditional notions of semantics and very heavily on the generative-transformational ideas of syntax found in N. Chomsky's *Syntactic Structures*.

Lyons' views on syntax, while on the whole clear and well formulated, can be criticized for (1) refusing to accord universal status to major grammatical categories such as "noun" and "verb" (here he follows the view of Robins in (1952); cf. pp. 67–69), although he is willing to consider certain grammatical operators, such as "negation," to be universally definable; (2) maintaining that designations such as "animate" or "personal" (of nouns) are not part of syntax but only of semantics, and that only the distributional characteristics of such nouns as fit these subclassifications are part of syntax (Lyons, 1963, p. 119, fn. 1); (3) maintaining that, in general, classification and subcategorization of categories should not be carried too far — "beyond the point of diminishing returns" (pp. 20–22, 137–138).

We have already discussed the first criticism in section 5 of this chapter. By maintaining the second notion, Lyons merely creates for himself a terminological inconvenience that he might just as well avoid. With the third, however, he lets himself in for serious difficulty. First he makes a point of not distinguishing grammatically such constructions as *colorless green ideas* from *revolutionary new ideas*, a position that has been amply criticized by Chomsky (1961), and for which no further discussion here is required. Moreover, Lyons is committed to the position that if, say, a verb and a noun appear morphologically to be related by a nominalization transformation, then *ipso facto* they are.

Now, I assume that the English forms *ignore* and *ignorance* could not be distinguished either phonologically or distributionally from other pairs of verbs and corresponding nouns that enter into the transformation [nominalization] mentioned here. Grammatically, therefore, *John's ignorance of this fact* is related to *John ignores this fact* precisely as *John's knowledge of this fact* is to *John knows this fact*. Semantically, of course, they are not. (p. 137)

The fact is that *ignore* and *ignorance* can be grammatically distinguished from *know* and *knowledge*, and so on, provided that one investigates details sufficiently "delicate" (to use Lyons' term) to reveal their difference. In this case, it is sufficient to notice that the putative nominalization of *John ignored this fact for purposes of the discussion* results in the ungrammatical phrase **John's ignorance of this fact for purposes of the discussion* in order to see that *ignorance* cannot be considered the nominalization of *ignore*. By disregarding such facts on the grounds that they are too "delicate," or beyond the point of diminishing returns, Lyons mistakes a problem concerning the incongruity between morphology and syntax as one between syntax and semantics (cf. Chomsky, 1964, p. 77 in Fodor and Katz, 1964).

Lyons' discussion of semantics, unlike that of most others of the London school, deals not only with the construction of a semantic theory but with the conditions of adequacy that any such theory must meet. The two major conditions of adequacy posed by Lyons are those of "operational" and "external" adequacy. Operational adequacy is the familiar condition imposed by positivists generally, and by taxonomic linguists in particular, for various scientific theories, which demands that their methods for obtaining hypothetical constructs be "operationally definable in terms of empirical techniques" (p. 11). On the basis of this condition, Lyons rules out, as one might expect, any "mentalistic" theory of semantics.

External adequacy, on the other hand, appears to correspond closely to Chomsky's "descriptive adequacy." It requires that semantics deal with the notions and issues raised within traditional semantics in an appropriate fashion, and it also requires that the theory be capable of "saving the appearances," or that it be compatible with "the known or apparent facts of language-learning and language use" (p. 7). In order to meet this condition, it must be capable of meeting what Katz and Fodor have called the "projection problem" for semantics. On the basis of external adequacy Lyons rejects Bloomfield's and also Osgood's theories of semantics, for they both fail to deal with what is ordinarily meant by "meaning."

Lyons does not raise the question whether it is possible or not to meet *both* conditions of adequacy with a single semantic theory. It is this author's belief that it is not, and that therefore operational conditions of adequacy should be dispensed with. We shall not defend this thesis here but shall simply examine whether in fact Lyons' semantic theory does or can meet external adequacy.

Lyons' theory is based on a fundamental distinction between the notions "having meaning" and "meaning (proper)." An utterance can be said to have meaning to the extent that it is *not* determined by context. (Lyons carefully distinguishes between "context" and "environment"; the latter is verbal context while the former is roughly Firth's context of situation — with some differences, as we shall see. We shall follow Lyons' uses of these terms in this discussion.) Utterances that are completely contextually determined therefore have no meaning, the semanticist's job in such cases being merely to record that these utterances occur. In defending this definition of "having meaning," Lyons makes it quite clear that he holds to what has been called the "use theory" of meaning and that there is no distinction between language and speech. In defending against the objection that no situation ever completely determines what will be said because all men are free not to say what is prescribed, he holds that "aberrations of use are no more part of the language than are aberrations of form" (p. 26). Thus, although Lyons takes what seems to be an opposite approach from Firth (context of situation eliminates meaning from utterances rather than supplying it), he is led to similar pronouncements concerning the proper use of language (compare especially the concluding discussion of Chapter 2).

Lyons recognizes that the fundamental problem of dealing with contexts of situation is that of identifying repetitions of contexts and of isolating significant elements from them. He is also aware that any simple identification of context with physical situation and with the personal histories of the participants is far from adequate. A description of semantically relevant contexts of situation, Lyons contends, must be based on the notion of "universe of discourse," which he defines, following W. M. Urban, as "the conventions and presuppositions maintained by 'the mutual acknowledgment of communicating subjects' in the particular type of linguistic behaviour under consideration" (p. 84). At this point Lyons takes pains to suggest that the notion is a bit "mentalistic" — he argues that since he does not "propose to look into the 'minds' of the speaker and hearer in order to situate the utterance in its context" (p. 86), the charge of mentalism is avoided. I am not convinced by this. For Lyons to determine these "conventions and presuppositions," he would presumably attempt to elicit from his informants responses that would reveal them. But what surety would Lyons have that embedded in his transcripts would be the relevant conventions and presuppositions, and how would he go about extracting them? These problems were not raised by him, but I think we can safely answer that a necessary condition for the relevance of such transcripts would be that they have some sort of coherence and rationality. Furthermore, to test whether the extracted presuppositions (presuming that certain ones could be extracted) were plausible, the investigator would doubtless have to weigh them *in his own mind*, even perhaps to project himself into the recreated situation so as to experience it vicariously. Thus the charge of mentalism is not avoided.

Since we have no particular brief against "mentalism," the fact that Lyons' form of "context of situation" turns out to be mentalistic in nature does not bother us; in fact, his identification of it with the notion "universe of discourse" seems quite plausible. It is noteworthy too that Lyons explicitly assigns to context of situation the role that properly belongs to it, namely, that of enabling the hearer to obtain the intended meaning of an utterance from the semantic content of it, and of enabling the speaker not to have to "mean what he says" at all times and in all places in order to be understood.

We turn now to Lyons' treatment of "meaning" itself. We shall consider separately what he has to say about substantive semantics and formal semantics (on these terms, cf. Chomsky, 1965, pp. 27–30).

Concerning substantive semantics, Lyons suggests that the categorial basis of definitions of items, using the familiar Aristotelian or post-Aristotelian notions of essense, property, genus, difference, and so on, should be replaced by what he terms "meaning-relations." As a paradigmatic case, he quotes H. Reichenbach's definition of the weight of a body as the class of all objects having the same weight as the body. The difficulty with such basically extensional definitions for semantic purposes (disregarding their possible value for strictly scientific purposes) should be readily apparent. In particular, they fail to meet his own sense of external adequacy, since it is a fact that people can distinguish quite readily between the intensionality and extensionality of a term, and will readily agree that the intensionality of a term is what is semantically significant. Lyons does, however, allow certain substantive categories to be used in forming definitions, but only when their reference is apparent (as in the case of the categories used to set up "componential analyses" of kinship terms). The distinction between referentially apparent and nonapparent categories is another reflection of Lyons' empiricist bias.

In the area of formal semantics Lyons is in a much stronger position. For reasons of external adequacy, he argues that any semantic theory must appropriately define and implement such traditional notions as "significance," "reference," "synonymy," "antonymy," "incompatibility," "analyticity" (although he hedges on this one, arguing in a footnote (p. 60) that this is more of a philosophical than a linguistic notion), "hyponymy" (the relation, for example, between *tulip* and *flower* in English), and "consequence" (the relationship, for example, between *manthánein* and *epístasthai* in Platonic Greek). Two serious criticisms, however, can be leveled against Lyons, one of a general nature and the other relating specifically to his treatment of synonymy.

The general criticism has to do with his treatment of "neutralization" of formal categories in relation to particular lexical items. For example, the relation of antonymy holds between *near* and *far* in English in many environments, but in the environment *How ——— is it?* the term *far* may appear without being antonymous with *near*. We may say that the antonymy has been neutralized in this environment. Following the London school principles that we have noted earlier in connection with phonological neutralization, Lyons suggests that *far* in the environment just mentioned belongs to a separate subsystem from *far* in those environments in which it is antonymous with *near* or, in other words, that it is a different lexical item from the other *far*. This kind of multiplication of items developed to handle instances of neutralization is totally unjustifiable, as we have already argued in connection with phonological neutralization.[11]

The notion of synonymy Lyons for some reason has chosen to consider as not on a par with the other formal semantic notions:

Finally, I may simply observe that synonymy is on a completely different level from the other meaning relations that have been discussed. (p. 77)

whereas in fact it is formally definable in terms of hyponymy. Thus *a* is synonymous with *b* in environment *c* if and only if *a* is hyponymous with *b* in *c* and *b* is hyponymous with *a* in *c*. Lyons' reason for segregating synonymy from the other formal notions is that he wishes to maintain that synonymy alone of the meaning relations is governed by context of situation. That is to say, two terms or expressions are synonymous in some context if we can show that the utterances in which they occur are acceptable to informants as "repetitions" of one another.

As an example, Lyons uses the sentences *We have a wide range of cigars* and *We have a wide selection of cigars*. Lyons insists that to test the synonymy of these utterances we must first select a suitable context, for example a buying-selling situation in a tobacconist's shop, and by ingenious questioning (which will not prejudice the case — no easy task!) determine whether cigar salesmen and customers would accept the two sentences as "repetitions" of each other. Lyons draws the parallel between this procedure and Harris' well-known "pair-test" for determining when two utterances are phonological repetitions; but the parallel is misleading in that Harris' test is relatively simple and straightforward while Lyons' is so hypothetical that it is even dubious whether it could ever be executed successfully.

A moment's reflection, however, should convince us that finding a suitable context and participants to play the "roles" is completely unnecessary. It is entirely likely that identical results could be achieved by questioning noncigar-smokers in an anechoic chamber. The only condition we would have to impose would be that we know in advance that the subjects understand the utterances.

Furthermore, modified versions of Lyons' procedure could equally well be used to test native speaker judgments about all the other formal semantic notions considered by Lyons to be important. For example, one could ask native speakers to tell us whether they would assent to

---

[11] The facts of neutralization noted by Lyons indicate quite strongly that the use of *features* plays a crucial role in semantic theory and description. Note also that syntax enters into consideration here too, inasmuch as the neutralization discussed by Lyons is really a grammatical fact with a concurrent semantic interpretation.

the truth of such propositions as *A tulip is a flower* (to test hyponymy), or, to use Lyons' own example (p. 89), *If X is single then X is married* (to test antonymy or incompatibility). We may conclude from these observations that synonymy is quite on a par with the other meaning relations, and that contexts of situation play absolutely no role in defining these notions.

4. Exemplifications of Prosodic Analysis

4.1 Introduction

In this chapter we shall undertake a careful study of a selected group of phonological analyses published by members of the London school over the period 1949–1962. In this study we shall attempt to make explicit the system of rules that is embodied in each of these descriptions. Wherever possible potential inadequacies of these descriptions will be pointed out, especially in those cases where it appears that generalizations about the language are being missed in the description. The interpretability of some of these descriptions in long-component terms will also be indicated.

The descriptions that have been selected for study here were chosen on the basis of their value for illustrating particular points and deficiencies of the prosodic approach, for their "accessibility" of interpretation, and for their intrinsic value as descriptions of the phonology of particular languages. In section 2, Henderson's description of Siamese will be considered (1949); in section 3, Allen's description of Sanskrit retroflexion (1951, 1954); in section 4, Allen's description of the Hāṛautī nominal (1957); in section 5, Allen's description of the Abaza verb (1956); in section 6, Carnochan's description of Hausa (1951, 1952, 1957); in section 7, Robins' description of Sundanese vowel nasality (1957); in section 8, Mitchell's description of accent in Arabic dialects

76

(1960); in section 9, Bendor-Samuel's description of Terena (1960, 1962); and in section 10, various papers by Palmer (1956), Waterson (1956), and Carnochan (1960) dealing with vowel harmony.

4.2 E. J. A. Henderson on Siamese (1949)

Henderson's prosodic description of Siamese phonology was one of the earliest attempts by a colleague of Firth's to exemplify his theory in an actual language study, and it has been referred to within the London school itself as "a typical type of phonological analysis on prosodic principles" (Bursill-Hall, 1961, p. 172). We have already commented upon Henderson's objective of achieving a "diagram" of the phonological relationships with Siamese (see earlier, p. 59) rather than a "reading transcription."

Henderson classified the prosodic features of Siamese into syllable-initial, syllable, word, and sentence prosodies, depending upon their domain. Her syllable-initial and syllable prosodies were set up to describe the distributional peculiarities of certain consonantal and vocalic features in the language, and as such may be viewed as long components. Henderson observed that the Siamese monosyllable can end only in nasal consonants, unreleased voiceless stops, semi-vowels, or vowels while the inventory of possible syllable-initial features is much larger.

It will be seen that plosion, aspiration, affrication, friction, voice (except when accompanied by nasality), and the presence of the sounds *r* or *l*, are properties of a syllable initial only, and mark the beginning of a syllable when they occur. These features . . . may be regarded as belonging to the prosodic system, while what is common to both syllable parts, initial and final, may be postulated as the consonantal system. (1949, p. 190)

The postulated consonant system contains the entities *p, t, k, m, n, ŋ*, and zero, and the syllable-initial prosodies (just listed) were considered to be added componentially to these phonematic units to form the syllable-initial sounds; *r* and *l* were considered to be the features "rhotacization" and "laterality" added to the zero consonant. Not all combinations of the prosodic features are, however, found in the language; and to describe this fact, Henderson simply listed the combinations that are permitted. The resulting description was simply an item-and-arrangement list of possible occurrences, and thus in a sense was weaker than a long-component description which defines the components in such a way that the nonoccurring combinations are excluded. We shall now give the context-sensitive "redundancy" rules corresponding to Henderson's analysis, and then give a long-component analysis of the consonant system of the monosyllable.

The "canonical" structure of the Siamese monosyllable may be expressed by the formula[1]

$$([+\text{cns}]) \left(\left\{ \begin{matrix} [+\text{cns}] \\ [-\text{voc}] \end{matrix} \right\} \right) [+\text{voc}]([+\text{voc}])([+\text{cns}])$$

The second position in the monosyllable may be occupied by either a glide or a liquid. Therefore, we have the rule:[2]

(1) $\left\{ \begin{matrix} [+\text{cns}] \\ {}_1[+\text{voc}] \end{matrix} \right\}_1 \rightarrow \left\{ \begin{matrix} [+\text{voc}] \\ {}_1[-\text{cns}] \end{matrix} \right\}_1 \Big/ [+\text{cns}] -$

The fourth position may be occupied by either a falling or a rising glide; curiously, Henderson treated the rising diphthongs as consisting of a vowel plus a prosody, but the falling diphthongs *iə, ɯə, uə* as unit phonematic units. The specification of these glides is given by the rules:

(2) $[+\text{voc}] \rightarrow [+\text{dff}] \Big/ \begin{bmatrix} +\text{voc} \\ -\text{dff} \end{bmatrix} -$

(3) $\begin{bmatrix} +\text{voc} \\ -\text{dff} \end{bmatrix} \rightarrow \begin{bmatrix} +\text{cmp} \\ -\text{flt} \\ +\text{grv} \end{bmatrix} \Big/ [+\text{voc}] -$

(4) $[+\text{voc}] \rightarrow [-\text{lng}] / - [+\text{voc}]$

By rules 2–4 we express the facts that only rising glides occur after nondiffuse vowels, falling glides are back unrounded, and that vowel length is neutralized in diphthongs.

The restrictions on the final consonant of the monosyllable are given by the rule:

---

[1] This formula may be considered an abbreviation for the morpheme structure rules (viewing the monosyllable as a morpheme for the purpose of the discussion) which supply the redundant features that can be predicted on the basis of the characteristic consonant-vowel patterns of morphemes.

[2] Rule 1 is an abbreviation for the separate rules:

(1*a*) $[+\text{cns}] \rightarrow [+\text{voc}]/[+\text{cns}] -$

and

(1*b*) $[+\text{voc}] \rightarrow [+\text{cns}]/[+\text{cns}] -$

(5) $\begin{bmatrix} +\text{cns} \\ -\text{nsl} \end{bmatrix} \rightarrow \begin{bmatrix} -\text{voc} \\ -\text{cnt} \\ -\text{voi} \\ -\text{tns} \\ -\text{std} \end{bmatrix} \Big/ - \#$

Single initial consonants are restricted according to the rules:

(6) $\begin{bmatrix} +\text{grv} \\ +\text{cmp} \end{bmatrix} \rightarrow \begin{bmatrix} -\text{voi} \\ -\text{cnt} \\ -\text{std} \end{bmatrix} \Big/ \,[\overline{+\text{cns}}][+\text{voc}]$

(7) $\begin{bmatrix} +\text{grv} \\ +\text{std} \end{bmatrix} \rightarrow [+\text{cnt}] / [\overline{+\text{cns}}][+\text{voc}]$

(8) $\left\{ \begin{matrix} [+\text{cnt}] \\ [+\text{voi}] \end{matrix} \right\} \rightarrow [-\text{tns}] / [\overline{+\text{cns}}][+\text{voc}]$

(9) $\left\{ \begin{matrix} [+\text{cnt}] \\ [+\text{std}] \end{matrix} \right\} \rightarrow [-\text{voi}] \Big/ \begin{bmatrix} \overline{+\text{cns}} \\ -\text{voc} \end{bmatrix} [+\text{voc}]$

Rule 6 specifies that there are no segments *x, g* parallel to *s, f* and to *d, b*.
Rule 7 specifies that there is no *pf* parallel to *č*; rule 8 that there are no
aspirated fricatives, nasals, liquids, or voiced stops parallel to *ph, th,
čh*, and *kh*; and rule 9 that there are no voiced fricatives or affricates.
These rules actually account for the features that are redundant as a
result of asymmetries in the consonantal inventory.

The following rules apply to initial clusters of consonant plus liquid
or glide:[3]

(10) $[+\text{cns}] \rightarrow \begin{bmatrix} -\text{voc} \\ -\text{cnt} \\ -\text{voi} \\ -\text{std} \\ -\text{nsl} \end{bmatrix} \Big/ \# - \left\{ \begin{matrix} [+\text{cns}] \\ [-\text{voc}] \end{matrix} \right\}$

(11) $[+\text{cns}] \rightarrow [+\text{flt}] / \# \begin{bmatrix} +\text{cns} \\ -\text{grv} \end{bmatrix} -$

[3] The α in rule 12 is a variable ranging over the values $+$ and $-$. Thus the rule
expresses the statement that a glide has the same gravity as the preceding consonant.
Rule 15 states simply that the elements 1 and 2 should be replaced with the element
1, which is further specified as being voiced and strident.

(12) $[-\text{voc}] \rightarrow \begin{bmatrix} -\text{cns} \\ \alpha\text{grv} \end{bmatrix} \bigg/ \# \begin{bmatrix} +\text{cns} \\ \alpha\text{grv} \end{bmatrix} -$

(13) $[+\text{grv}] \rightarrow [+\text{cmp}] / \# \overline{[+\text{cns}]} \begin{bmatrix} -\text{voc} \\ -\text{cns} \end{bmatrix}$

(14) $\begin{bmatrix} +\text{cns} \\ -\text{grv} \end{bmatrix} \rightarrow [-\text{tns}] / \# - \begin{Bmatrix} [+\text{cns}] \\ [-\text{voc}] \end{Bmatrix}$

(15) $\begin{bmatrix} +\text{cns} \\ -\text{grv} \end{bmatrix} \begin{bmatrix} -\text{cns} \\ -\text{grv} \end{bmatrix}$

$$1 \qquad 2 \ \rightarrow \begin{bmatrix} 1 \\ +\text{voi} \\ +\text{std} \end{bmatrix} \phi$$

Rule 10 specifies that only voiceless stops may precede a liquid or a glide; rule 11 that the sequences *tl* and *thl* are excluded; rules 13 and 14 that *kw*, *khw*, and *ty* are the only combinations of consonant and glide that are found, and that *thr* is excluded; and rule 15 that *ty* is pronounced [ǰ].

The segment [ǰ], alternatively, might be considered to represent a voiced counterpart to *č*, in which case rule 9 would be simplified to

(9) $[+\text{cnt}] \rightarrow [-\text{voi}]/\overline{[-\text{voc}]}$

This analysis would also make *kw* and *khw* the only consonant plus glide combinations in the language, suggesting the possibility that they might be treated as single segments, distinguishable from *k* and *kh* by, say, the feature of flatness. This decision would result in a simplification of the specification of the canonical structure of the monosyllable; we would be able to write it as

$$[+\text{cns}]^2[+\text{voc}]_1^2[+\text{cns}]^1$$

One feature, flatness, however, would have to be added to the right-hand side of rule 10.

Following *kw* and *khw*, only the front vowels and *a* are permitted, so we require a rule:

(16) $[+\text{voc}] \rightarrow \begin{Bmatrix} [-\text{grv}] \\ \begin{bmatrix} +\text{cmp} \\ -\text{flt} \end{bmatrix} \end{Bmatrix} \bigg/ \begin{bmatrix} -\text{cns} \\ -\text{voc} \\ +\text{grv} \end{bmatrix} -$

The second element of rising diphthongs is restricted according to the rule

$$(17) \quad [-\text{cns}] \rightarrow \begin{bmatrix} -\alpha\text{grv} \\ -\alpha\text{flt} \end{bmatrix} \Big/ \begin{bmatrix} \alpha\text{grv} \\ \left\{ \begin{matrix} -\text{cmp} \\ +\text{flt} \end{matrix} \right\} \end{bmatrix} [+\text{dff}]$$

The diphthongs *iw, ew, wi, ɤi, uy, oy*, and so on, are permitted, as are both *ay* and *aw*. The second member of a diphthong is nonsyllabic; therefore,

$$(18) \quad [\ \ ] \rightarrow [-\text{voc}]/[+\text{voc}] —$$

The following long components are sufficient to handle the restrictions on consonant sequences in initial position: (1) a component ——— defined as nonflatness and nonaspiration over initial consonant sequences beginning with an alveolar stop, (2) a component == defined as sameness of gravity of initial sequences of consonant plus glide, and (3) a component ** defined as voiceless plosion and nonnasality defined over initial consonant clusters (having no effect on the second member). This same component, but without the restriction on nasality, may be said to be associated with the end of the monosyllable.

Henderson's very brief description of tone in Siamese is also largely a description of redundancy features. Each syllable, with the restrictions to be noted in a moment, may bear one of five tones, which may be roughly described as mid-level, low-level, rising, falling, and rising-falling. These five tones may be distinguished by the three binary features low, rise, and fall. The restrictions on the occurrence of tone may be stated as:

$$(19) \quad [+\text{voc}] \rightarrow \left\{ \begin{matrix} \begin{bmatrix} -\text{ris} \\ -\text{fal} \end{bmatrix} \\ {}_1[+\text{low}] \end{matrix} \right\}_1 \Big/ \left\{ \begin{matrix} [+\text{lng}] \\ {}_1[-\text{lng}] \end{matrix} \right\}_1 \begin{bmatrix} +\text{cns} \\ -\text{nsl} \end{bmatrix} \#$$

$$(20) \quad \left\{ \begin{matrix} \begin{bmatrix} -\text{grv} \\ -\text{dff} \end{bmatrix} \\ \begin{bmatrix} +\text{grv} \\ +\text{cmp} \end{bmatrix} \end{matrix} \right\} \rightarrow [\alpha\text{lng}] \Big/ \begin{bmatrix} +\text{voc} \\ \alpha\text{ris} \end{bmatrix}$$

Rule 19 specifies that only level tone is found on long vowels before a stop, and only falling or low-level tone occurs on short vowels before a stop. According to rule 20 the tone on the vowels *e, æ,* and *ɔ* will be rising when the vowel is long and not rising when the vowel is short. There is also at least a historical connection between the aspiration of a preceding consonant and the tone of a vowel.

Henderson also, however, described certain phonological phenomena in Siamese that can only be interpreted by rules which change inherent features or delete inherent segments. All of these rules apply in either compound words or polysyllabic words. In compounds, where each member is a monosyllable, the tone of the first syllable is changed according to tonal sandhi rules, which Henderson exemplifies — but not sufficiently for the corresponding rules to be stated for certain. She does state clearly, however, that if the first member of the compound ends in a long vowel, that vowel is shortened, but whether its phonetic length can be distinguished from the length of an inherently short vowel is open to question. If not, then the rule that shortens these vowels can be stated simply as[4]

(21) $[+\text{voc}] \rightarrow [-\text{lng}]/ - \# [\quad]$

In certain compounds, however, an extra syllable appears that is not found with either of the simple words making it up. Thus, for example, `ra:t "king" plus ¯ja:n "vehicle" yields the compound `ra:tčha¯ja:n "palanquin," where the middle syllable has "neutral tone." There are many such compounds, and in each of them a distinctive middle syllable appears. This syllable must be considered a part of the first member of the compound; in this example, the word for "king" must be lexically represented as `ra:tčha. But if this is so, then there must be a rule that deletes the last syllable of such words when it is not compounded:

(22) $CV \rightarrow \phi/\#\#CVC - \#\#$

Rule 22 applies only to words of Sanskrit or Pali origin, so presumably such words will have to be marked distinctively in the lexicon as undergoing rule 22.

The structure of Siamese polysyllables is such that the rules given so far do not have to be changed significantly to cover them. The permitted medial clusters of consonants include those made up of stops or nasals followed by any of the consonants or consonant clusters permitted by rules 10–14.

A further rule governing tone in polysyllabic words and in compounds neutralizes the tone of all vowels that are inherently short and are followed by no more than one consonant (optionally followed by a glide or liquid) and another vowel; for brevity, we shall refer to these vowels as occurring in weak syllables. The tone found on all these syl-

---

[4] We adopt the convention that the two parts of compound words are separated by a single word boundary. When two independent words come together, they will be separated by two word boundaries.

lables is called "neutral tone" and is approximately that of the mid-
level tone in quality. We can express this fact by means of the rule

$$(23) \quad \begin{bmatrix} +\text{voc} \\ -\text{lng} \end{bmatrix} \rightarrow \begin{bmatrix} -\text{low} \\ -\text{ris} \\ -\text{fal} \end{bmatrix} \Big/ -(\#)[+\text{cns}]^1 \begin{bmatrix} \alpha\text{cns} \\ \alpha\text{voc} \end{bmatrix}^1 [+\text{voc}]$$

As we have stated them, rule 21 must follow rule 23 so as to prevent
the complete neutralization of tone on long vowels that are final in the
first word of compounds. If, however, the length of these vowels can
be distinguished from that of inherently short vowels, the problem of
ordering does not arise.

It will be noted that the neutral tone on the medial syllable in compounds originating from Sanskrit or Pali follows automatically from
rule 23. It may be no accident that the weak syllable figures prominently
in the tonal system of both Siamese and Indo-European; it may prove
worth while to investigate the historical implications of this identity of
environment in the tonal rules of the two language families involved.

Henderson pointed out that rules 21 and 23 operate only in certain
styles of speaking, namely, nondeliberate or ordinary conversational
styles. In deliberate or slow speech, vowel length and inherent tone is
preserved. These facts were used by Henderson so that she could avoid
having to say that rules 21 and 23 apply at all and instead could say
that there are two styles of speech, or two "languages" if you will, that
are related by these rules. Thus, Henderson was able to maintain a
strictly classificatory phonological description of Siamese; she was able
to rule out precisely those rules which change inherently specified features. The cost for having done so, however, is considerable. Since,
technically, each language requires a separate description, the total
number of rules to describe the two speech styles viewed as separate
languages will be about twice the number required to describe them
as one. To account for the two speech styles in such a "monosystemic"
description, we need simply state that rules 21 and 23 are optional: if
they are applied, then ordinary colloquial style is described; if not, then
deliberate or slow style is described.

4.3 W. S. Allen on Sanskrit (1951, 1954)

Allen's prosodic treatment of the well-known Sanskrit "rule of cere-
bralization" [5] is important because it is often cited as proof that state-

---

[5] Cf. A. A. MacDonnell (1916, p. 9): "The cerebral *ṇ* appears within a word only
. . . replacing dental *n* after *r*, *ṛ* or *ṣ* (either immediately preceding or separated
from it by certain intervening letters)."

ments involving concepts like assimilation are avoided in prosodic description; thus Robins has remarked:

> A prosodic restatement of the familiar Sanskrit rule of 'cerebralization' has been made by setting up in the words concerned a word prosody or word part prosody of retroflexion (R), thereby avoiding the rather tiresome concept of 'action at a distance' of one sound on another in traditional accounts. (1963, p. 30)

Allen's description aims to associate with the phonematic units *l* and *s* a prosody of retroflexion whose domain extends forward, toward the end of a word, to include either all segments that are not dentals, up to and including the word boundary, or a dental, whichever comes first. The exponents of the prosody are, first, retroflexion of its focus (to yield either *r* or *ṣ*), and second, retroflexion of the last segment in its domain if that is a nasal. This description, however, can hardly be called anything but a notational variant of the traditional description; one which in fact obscures the fact that an underlying *n* is assimilated to *ṇ* by a preceding retroflex consonant, as in, for example, *brahmaṇa*.

The segment *ṣ*, which is a focus of Allen's retroflexion prosody, arises from an underlying nonretroflex *s* according to the rule

$$(1) \quad \begin{bmatrix} +\text{std} \\ -\text{cmp} \end{bmatrix} \rightarrow [+\text{flt}] \; / \; \left\{ \begin{bmatrix} \begin{bmatrix} +\text{voc} \\ +\text{dff} \end{bmatrix} \\ \begin{bmatrix} +\text{cns} \\ +\text{cmp} \\ +\text{grv} \end{bmatrix} \end{bmatrix} \right\} \; —$$

This is to say that *s* is retroflex when it follows either a diffuse vowel or *k* as, for example, in *cakṣuṣ, gauṣaṇi* "winning cattle."

Rule 1 must be considered to apply before the rule that corresponds to Allen's retroflexion prosody, which, as we have remarked, must be stated as a rule that does involve assimilation:

$$(2) \quad \begin{bmatrix} +\text{nsl} \\ -\text{grv} \end{bmatrix} \rightarrow [+\text{flt}] \; / \; \begin{bmatrix} +\text{cns} \\ +\text{flt} \end{bmatrix} \left\{ \begin{matrix} [-\text{cns}] \\ \left\{ \begin{matrix} [+\text{grv}] \\ [+\text{cmp}] \end{matrix} \right\} \end{matrix} \right\}_0 \; — [-\text{obs}]$$

However, there are exceptions to this rule, for example, *pranankṣyati;* by rule 2, we would expect to find **praṇankṣyati*.[6] As Allen pointed out, all these exceptions are of the type where the nasal that is not retroflexed according to rule is followed by a second retroflex consonant. To account for this phenomenon in prosodic terms, Allen sug-

---

[6] These exceptions are extremely rare, and all have to do with the presence of *r* in a preverb.

gested that the *n* in question acts as a sort of "boundary" between the retroflexion prosodies associated with, in this case, the *r* of the prefix *pra-* and the *ṣ* and as such is outside the domain of either of them:

> On the basis of this method of statement it might be argued that the interrupting nasal articulation then bears to the two R-prosodies much the same relationship as a prosodic syllable marker . . . bears to the two syllables; and hence that as the syllable marker belongs to a different dimension from the linear syllables, so the "prosody-separator" must belong to yet another dimension outside that of the R-prosodies themselves. We need not be afraid to admit such a possibility: rather we should be prepared to add to our analytical framework just as many dimensions as the material demands. (1951, p. 946)

Just what Allen's appeal to dimensionality was supposed to mean is difficult to assess.

4.4 W. S. Allen on Hārautī (1957)

We have already discussed Allen's paper "Aspiration in the Hārautī Nominal" in the preceding chapter in terms of the formal character of his prosodic description. Here we shall discuss its content. Allen himself supplied a convenient summary of the phonological facts that he wished to provide descriptions of:

> (i) A breathy transition is never followed or preceded by another breathy transition within the word.
> (ii) A voiceless articulation is never followed by a breathy transition except immediately (i.e. when the voiceless articulation in question forms the prior term of the transition).
> (iii) Within the above restrictions, breathy transitions from voiceless articulations are found either initially or non-initially; but by (ii) such non-initial transitions imply that no other voiceless articulation precedes.
> (iv) Breathy transitions other than from a voiceless articulation are only found initially. (1957, p. 72)

It is clear that it is possible to provide a straightforward taxonomic phonemic analysis of these facts, and Allen in fact conveniently provided such an analysis (pp. 81–83). The one he gave looks just like a paraphrase of the facts given, especially the statement of "defective distribution," which reads (paralleling (i) to (iii)):

> (a) Aspirated /C/ implies unaspirated following /C/ and preceding /C/.
> (b) Voiceless /C/ implies unaspirated following /C/.
> (c) Aspirated /C/ implies voiced preceding /C/. (p. 83)

Allen, however, rejected this statement on the grounds that a statement of the distribution of phonemes is necessitated only by the

assumption that the basic phonological entities are invariant phonemes
— precisely Harris' argument in 1944 (see my discussion in Chapter 3,
pp. 54–56).

Allen also rejected as inappropriate any description involving the
notions of assimilation or dissimilation of features, but here as in the
case of Sanskrit retroflexion, he had no substantive argument; the rules
governing the facts of Hāṛautī aspiration (where we use the feature
tenseness to distinguish the aspirates from the nonaspirates) may be
expressed as follows (cf. Langendoen, 1964, pp. 319–320):

(1) $[+\text{voi}] \rightarrow [-\text{tns}]/[\ \ ] -$

(2) $[\ \ ] \rightarrow [-\text{tns}] \Big/ \begin{Bmatrix} [+\text{tns}] \\ [-\text{voi}] \end{Bmatrix} [\ \ ]_{\text{o}} -$

Since Allen's prosodic analysis may be regarded merely as a complicated notation that expresses the same thing as these two rules, he
would have no basis for rejecting them as "inappropriate."

Within Allen's descriptive framework, rules 1 and 2 must be viewed
as redundancy rules; thus they meet the restriction that they be classificatory in nature. Whether or not in a phonological description of the
entire language, they must be viewed otherwise, that is, as possibly
changing the specification of otherwise-specified segments, cannot be
determined from Allen's paper, since he provided no illustrative material that could possibly bear on the question. It would be interesting to
know what "morphophonemic" alternations take place in the language,
so that one could determine whether the historical development of
"throwing back of aspiration" is still preserved as a rule in the syn-
chronic description. The historical development was summarized by
Allen:

The voiced aspirates and *h* are only tolerated initially; in other cases the
(inherited) aspiration is either dropped or, if a voiceless unaspirated stop
precedes, is thrown back upon it to produce a voiceless aspirate. Even voiceless aspirates are eschewed in non-initial position if a voiceless stop or *s* precedes; and if such preceding stop is unaspirated, the aspiration is thrown back
upon it as from voiced aspirates. (p. 86)

A rule embodying the historical development may be expressed simply
as follows:

(3) $[-\text{voi}] \rightarrow [+\text{tns}]/ - [\ \ ]_{\text{o}}[+\text{tns}]$

If there happen to be morphophonemic alternations, say of the type
that when *dha* is added to the stem *ka* the resulting form is *khada*, then

rule 3 would have to be considered part of the phonological component of Hāṛautī, rules 1 and 2 would not be simply redundancy rules in that component, and Allen's contention that the historical of all the possible phonological descriptions is "at once the most concise and the least appropriate of all" (p. 70) would be false, at least as far as appropriateness is concerned.

4.5 W. S. Allen on Abaza (1956)

Allen's description of the phonology of the Abaza verb must rank as one of the most fascinating and thoroughgoing phonological analyses to be published recently. Allen took a very sharply and somewhat artificially delimited part of the language as his data, namely, verb complexes that can function as independent sentences. Interrogative forms of the verb are also excluded, but a large number of examples of them are scattered throughout the paper. The fact that the analysis does not integrate at all with a description of the rest of the language's phonology must be considered the most serious drawback of the whole study.

The verbal complex, the constituents of which include the verb root, concord or agreement elements, tense and aspect elements, and optionally such constituents as preverbs, and negative, interrogative, directional, causative, and potential elements, always contains just one stressed vowel, and there is just a two-way phonological contrast in the quality of that vowel. Allen symbolized these vowels as *a* (relatively open) and *ə* (relatively close); we may consider that it is the feature compactness that distinguishes them. The actual phonetic quality of these vowels varies widely, depending upon their context, but in the same environment *ə* is generally relatively closer than *a*. Before the semivowels *y* and *w*, the vowels *a* and *ə* take on the gravity of the semivowel, and are raised in tongue height, so that before *y*, *a* is pronounced approximately [e] and *ə* is approximately [i]. In word-initial position, however, *ay* and *aw* are pronounced [ay] and [aw], respectively. The statement of the phonetic qualities of the two vowels in other contexts is similarly straightforward.

Relatively unstressed vowels also occur in verbal complexes, and the quality of these vowels may also be distinguished simply on the basis of the feature compactness. Moreover, the position of the noncompact vowels can, for the most part, be predicted and so need not be represented in the phonological transcription. Interestingly enough, although Allen called these insertable vowels "prosodic," he also spoke of them as being introduced by rules, governed by rather complex conditions, which he had not succeeded in working out at the time of the publication of the paper:

These conditions are highly complex, and a comprehensive statement has yet to be evolved; the most widely applicable is the 'two-consonant rule', which must however be understood as subject to restriction by other conflicting rules (concerned in particular with the sem-vocalic, liquid and nasal articulations); the rule is statable as follows: —
Counting the consonantal articulations back from the end of the complex, or from any vocalic articulation bearing main or secondary stress, there is a secondarily stressed vocalic transition between the second and third consonantal articulations. (1956, p. 142)

The "two-consonant rule" can be expressed as follows:[7]

$$(1) \quad \phi \to \begin{bmatrix} +\text{voc} \\ -\text{cns} \\ -\text{cmp} \\ -\text{acc} \end{bmatrix} \Big/ \ C_1 - (C_2^2)_1 \left\{ \begin{matrix} \# \\ \begin{bmatrix} +\text{voc} \\ -\text{cns} \end{bmatrix} \end{matrix} \right\}$$

It follows, therefore, that if the position of the noncompact unstressed vowels can be predicted by rule, there is no contrast in the quality of those unstressed vowels whose position is not predictable. Their quality will always be compact:

From these considerations it follows that close vocalic articulations in other than the main stressed syllable are to be treated as prosodic ("anaptyctic") and not as phonematic; so that in such syllables only a one-term vowel-system is establishable, having openness as the exponent of its single term. (p. 142)

That is to say, prior to the application of rule 1, there is a rule

$$(2) \quad \begin{bmatrix} +\text{voc} \\ -\text{cns} \\ -\text{acc} \end{bmatrix} \to [+\text{cmp}]$$

It can, however, be shown that the assertion embodied in rule 2, that the quality of the unstressed vowels in Abaza verbs can always be predicted, is false, on the basis of evidence supplied by Allen himself. To show this, we must first point out that the placement of stress in verbal complexes is at least partially predictable — a consideration not raised

---

[7] Since for purposes of the discussion only vowels with main stress or secondary stress are being considered, we may designate secondary stressed vowels as being unstressed.

by Allen. First consider the form[8] *drʃy'əd* "they killed him/her," which has the morphological composition:

(i)   *d*   *r*   *ʃyə*   *d*
      he/she they Root Aspect

as opposed to the form *dgyrz'əmʃyd* "they couldn't kill him/her," which has the composition:

(ii)   *d*   *gy*   *r*   *zə*   *m*   *ʃyə*   *d*
       he/she Negative they Potential Negative Root Aspect

Comparison of these two forms reveals that in form ii, the underlying *ə* of the root *ʃyə* was deleted. If we suppose that in form ii the stress assignment rule first assigned main stress to the *ə* of *zə*, the potential constituent, then we may suppose that a later rule deleted the unstressed *ə* of *ʃyə*. In form i, since the *ə* of *ʃyə* received the main stress by the stress assignment rule (being the only vowel in the form), it was not deleted. In fact, however, not all unstressed underlying *ə*'s are deleted in Abaza, but only those *ə*'s which are morpheme final. For this reason, the *ə* of the verbal root *əs* "hit" is never deleted, even when unstressed. Thus, we have the forms *dy'əsd* "he/she hit him" and *danb'ayəs* "when did he/she hit him?" with the morphological composition:

(iii)   *d*   *y*   *əs*   *d*
        he/she he Root Aspect

and

(iv)   *d*   *anba*   *y*   *əs*
       he/she Interrogative he Root

One may contrast with form iv the form (with the root *əs*) *danb'ayʃy* "when did he kill him/her?" which has the composition:

(v)   *d*   *anba*   *y*   *ʃyə*
      he/she Interr. he Root

The fact that nonmorpheme final *ə*'s are never deleted, even when unstressed, means that there is a systematic exception to Allen's contention that the quality of unstressed vowels, whose occurrence is not predictable by the anaptyxis rule(s), is predictable by rule 2. It will be noted that in form iv the position of the unstressed *ə* would not be pre-

---

[8] For typographical convenience, we have altered slightly Allen's orthography in our Abaza citations. Main stress is indicated with a mark preceding the vowel. All *y* and *w* are written on the line.

dicted correctly by the anaptyxis rule 1. If, however, we should decide to drop rule 2 from the phonological component of Abaza, and maintain instead that the two-way opposition of vowel quality is maintained in both accented and unaccented positions, and that there is a rule which deletes morpheme-final unstressed ə's, then the occurrence of ə in form iv and similar forms is no longer to be considered exceptional. This way of formulating the rules of the language also makes it easy to state the rules of stress placement, whereas in Allen's formulation it would be impossible to state them, since the position of stress (for the correct application of rule 2) would have to be considered phonemic. Unfortunately, it is not possible to determine the rules of stress assignment from Allen's description; since his paper is not oriented toward the problem, the crucial examples are not discussed.

The rule of ə-deletion may be stated as follows:

$$(3) \quad \begin{bmatrix} +\text{voc} \\ -\text{cns} \\ -\text{cmp} \\ -\text{acc} \end{bmatrix} \rightarrow \phi / -\!+$$

Other examples that illustrate the application of rule 3 are *yʃytʔ'əlxd* "she lifted it," from the underlying form:

(vi) y   ʃytʔə   l   xə   d
     it Preverb she Root Asp.

and *yʃytʔn'axd* "it lifted it," from the form:

(vii) y   ʃytʔə   na   xə   d
      it Preverb it Root Asp.

It will be noted as a further justification of the formulation of the rules presented here, as opposed to Allen's formulation, that by considering unstressed underlying ə's as deleted, we can represent a form like the preverb *ʃytʔə* in the underlying representation uniquely, whereas Allen would be obliged to represent it sometimes as *ʃytʔ*, as he does for example in form vii, and sometimes as *ʃytʔə*, as he does in form vi.

In section 3 of his paper, Allen discussed some extraordinarily intricate phonological phenomena involving junction in the verbal radical. The first of these concerns the voicing of the concord forms *s* "first singular," *h* "first plural," and *ʃw* "second plural"; these forms are voiced when they precede a verb root initial voiced obstruent, and when they themselves are not word initial. This is the case also when the element *m*, which is part of the negative constituent, intervenes between the concord form and the radical. If we designate the concord form by the symbol P, we may express the rule which voices these forms as[9]

$$(4) \quad [\quad] \rightarrow [+\text{voi}]/[\quad] + [_P\!\!-\!\!_P](+m) + [_{\text{Root}} \begin{bmatrix} +\text{obs} \\ +\text{voi} \end{bmatrix}$$

Rule 4 does not have any effect on the other concord forms besides the three listed, since they consist of segments that are inherently voiced. Allen remarked that since only the class of obstruents is distinctively voiced in Abaza, the voicing can be said to occur before radicals whose initial segment is distinctively voiced.

The second instance of junctural phenomena that Allen discussed concerned the third plural concord form r, which dissimilates to d before the causative morpheme r, root-initial r, and itself. It also dissimilates to d before the morpheme *ara* to form the "disjunctive pronoun" *dara* "they" (the parallel forms s "first person" plus *ara* yields *sara* "I," and so on). Any constituent may intervene between the concord form and the following form containing an r, except apparently preverbs (to explain Allen's example 77). The rule of dissimilation can be expressed simply as

$$(5) \quad [+\text{cns}] \rightarrow \begin{bmatrix} -\text{voc} \\ -\text{flt} \end{bmatrix} \Big/ [_P\!\!-\!\!_P] \, X \begin{bmatrix} +\text{cns} \\ +\text{voc} \\ +\text{flt} \end{bmatrix}$$

where X does not contain a preverb or $\#$. If we assume that preverbs occur with a word boundary, that is, we treat them as enclitics, then rule 5 can be simplified in an obvious way.

Next, Allen observed that if a verbal root begins with a ∂, it metathesizes with an immediately preceding m, which is part of the negation constituent. Thus from underlying

(viii) s gy l m ∂s d
    I Neg. she Neg. Root Asp.

we get the form *sgyl'∂msd* "I didn't hit her." If the causative r, however, intervenes between the m and the root, the metathesis is blocked:

(ix) s gy l y m r ∂s d
    I Neg. she he Neg. Causative Root Asp.

[9] Brackets labeled with grammatical categories such as P or Root enclose the forms that designate those grammatical categories. Both left and right brackets are labeled, whence the two P's in rule 4.

is pronounced *sgylymr'əsd* "he didn't make me hit her." If, however, the complex contains three concord elements, and there is no causative constituent to block the metathesis, the third concord element along with *m* metathesizes with the radical-initial *ə*. Thus from

(x)   *y   gy   l   zə   s   m   əʒw   d*
       it Neg. she Pot. I Neg. Root Asp.

we get *ygylz'əsmʒwd* "I couldn't drink it for her," by metathesis of the *ə* of the root *əʒw* "drink" with the preceding constituents *s* and *m*, and deletion of the unaccented *ə* of *zə* by rule 3. In a similar manner, from

(xi)   *y   l   s   ət   d*
        it she I Root Asp.

we get *yl'əstd* "I gave it to her." We may express the *ə*-metathesis rule as follows, where P_3 indicates the third concord element in the verbal complex:

(6) $X_1 + (P_3) + (m) + [_{\text{Root}} \; ə, \; X_2]_{\text{Root}}$
        1   2   3   4   5 $\rightarrow$ 1   4 + 2   3 ϕ 5

Transformational notation has been used to express rule 6, even though it is a phonological rule. This notation is a simple and natural way to express phonological metathesis, which may be viewed as the phonological counterpart to syntactical permutation. Actually, permutation (and metathesis) is properly expressed as a combination of the simpler operations of adjunction and deletion; as we have stated rule 6, it will be seen that both these operations have been expressed: the *ə* (element 4) has been adjoined in front of element 2, and also deleted in its original position. If rule 6 is made to precede rule 4, then we account correctly for the fact that, if upon metathesis a concord element immediately precedes a voiced obstruent that is radical initial (although that obstruent is not radical initial in the underlying form), with an optionally intervening *m*, that element is voiced (p. 148). Thus, for example, the element *s* in form x is voiced.

We are now in a position to explain a particular phonetic ambiguity that Allen noted but did not (or could not) explain. The form *ygylz'əsmʒwd*, with the verb root *əʒw*, is derived from form x, as we have seen, by application of rules 6, 4, and 3 in that order. This form also may result, however, from an underlying form in which the verb root is *ʒwə* "boil," namely the form:

(xii)   *y   gy   l   zə   s   m   ʒwə   d*
        it Neg. she Pot. I Neg. Root Asp.

By stress assignment, stress is placed on the vowel ə of *zə*. By rule 4 the concord element *s* is voiced, and by rule 3 the unaccented ə of *ʒwə* is deleted, resulting in *ygylz'əsmʒwd*, as before. Thus we see that the phonetic ambiguity of this form results from the application of different phonological rules to different underlying representations. Since Allen made no attempt to formalize the rules of "juncture," and since he had no way of accounting for the appearance and disappearance of ə in the morphemes *zə* and *ʒwə*, he was unable to see why this ambiguity should have arisen.

From these two examples, forms x and xii, we see, incidentally, that the stress-assignment rules might have the following property: if the verbal complex contains two morpheme-final ə's, as in form xii, the first receives the main stress; if, as in form x, the second ə is not morpheme final, it receives the main stress.

The final "junction" phenomenon noted by Allen concerned the pronunciation of the diphthongs *ay* and *aw* in certain positions. As we have already noted (on p. 87), noninitial *ay* and *aw* should be pronounced [ey] and [ow], respectively. There are certain forms, however, where, like *əy* and *əw*, they are pronounced [iy] and [uw]. Forms in which this pronunciation is found all have certain grammatical characteristics, listed by Allen in his description (p. 151), and there does not seem to be any obvious way to improve upon this description despite its inelegance.

It is interesting to note that Allen described *none* of these juncture phenomena in prosodic terms, and that furthermore, if he did, it would weaken his description. Take, for instance, the last phenomenon he described, namely, the "neutralization" of *ay* and *aw* with *əy* and *əw* in certain contexts. Despite the identical pronunciations of these diphthongs, Allen kept them phonologically distinct in his representation. In a prosodic description, however, he would be unable to keep them distinct, precisely because a prosodic description involves allotting *phonetic* data to prosodic elements. Since the only phonetic data in these contexts are the forms [iy] and [uw], there is no way open for him to maintain the distinction between compact and noncompact vowels in those contexts. But clearly, in an adequate description, the distinction must be maintained, so as to reveal the correct paradigmatic relationships in a single conjugation, if nothing else.

In section 4 of his paper, Allen discussed certain grammatical characteristics of the Abaza verb. The verbal complex contains up to three positions or slots in front of the verb root for which concord elements may be substituted, and following Allen for the time being we may designate them as P_1, P_2, and P_3. Seven different concord elements, exclusive of the relative, reflexive, and reciprocal elements, which are not discussed in the paper, may be substituted for P_1, and nine may be substituted for both P_2 and P_3. The forms for the third person masculine and feminine singular, and for the third person nonhuman and plural, which are distinct in P_2 and P_3, are collapsed into one form apiece in P_1. Instead of a concord element, a noun may appear in the P_1 position if it is either nonhuman or plural (pp. 133–134).

Verbs with a single object fall into two classifications, according to whether P_1 is in concord with the subject or with the object, and vice versa for P_2. If we designate these classes as 1 and 2 (in the inverse order, following Allen), we require a classificatory rule:[10]

(C.1) $P_1 P_2 \, X \, \text{Verb}_{\{1, 2\}} \rightarrow P_{\{o, s\}} \, P_{\{s, o\}} \, X \, \text{Verb}_{\{1, 2\}}$

Verbs in class C.1, however, take the order of agreement $P_s P_o$ in reciprocal sentences.

There would be no need for such a rule if we supposed that the concord positions were designated as subject-agreeing and object-agreeing from the start. If we take the order $P_s P_o$ as fundamental, then we could derive the order of the concord elements with verbs of class C.1 by means of the following transformational rule:

(T.1) $\begin{array}{ccccc} P_s \, P_o \, X \, \text{Verb}_1 \\ 1 \ \ 2 \ \ 3 \ \ \ 4 \ \ \rightarrow \phi \ \ \ \ 2 \ \ \ \ 1+3 \ \ \ \ 4 \ \ \ \ \text{if } P_o \neq \text{Reciprocal} \end{array}$

From the examples given by Allen, it appears that all verbs that occur with two objects, such as *ət* "give," are of class C.1. We may designate the concord element in agreement with the indirect object as P_i. The analysis that considers as fundamental the functional designations P_s and P_o for the concord positions, rather than the sequence designations P_1 and P_2, receives further justification from the fact that it is the functional designations that are used in the statement of other transformational rules of the language. For example, any verbal prefix (or preverb) follows P_o, regardless of its position relative to P_s, according to the rule:

(T.2) $\begin{array}{ccc} P_o \, X \, \text{Preverb} \\ 1 \ \ 2 \ \ \ 3 \ \ \rightarrow 1+3 \ \ \ \ 2 \ \ \ \ \phi \end{array}$

The constituent that Allen called "Potential" follows P_s, regardless of its position relative to P_o; thus:

[10] Note that this is not a transformation rule as such. Classificatory rules may be considered to be a special kind of lexical rule, and apply together with the other lexical rules after the phrase-structure expansion rules.

$$\text{(T.3)} \quad \frac{P_s \; X \text{ Potential}}{1 \; 2 \quad 3} \quad \rightarrow 1 + 3 \quad 2 \quad \phi$$

We shall not be concerned for the time being about where the constituents Preverb and Potential are located prior to the application of rules T.2 and T.3; we shall now discuss further the problem of stating the phrase structure of the Abaza verb, which, of course, bears on this question.

Causative verbal forms are formed from simple ones by prefixing a causative element to the verb root. The agent of the cause is indicated by a concord element that is located directly before the causative morpheme, and we shall designate that concord element as P_a. With the class C.1 verb root *ʃyə* "kill" we have the simple form:

$$\text{(xiii)} \quad \frac{y \; l \; \text{ʃyə} \; d}{P_o \, P_s \text{ Root Asp.}}$$

ylʃy'əd "she killed it." A corresponding causative is:

$$\text{(xiv)} \quad \frac{y \; l \; s \; r \; \text{ʃyə} \; d}{P_o \, P_s \, P_a \text{ Caus. Root Asp.}}$$

ylsrʃy'əd "I made her kill it." With the class C.2 verb root *əs* "hit," we have the simple verbal form:

$$\text{(xv)} \quad \frac{d \; r \; \text{əs} \; d}{P_s \, P_o \text{ Root Asp.}}$$

dr'əsd "he/she hit them." A corresponding causative is

$$\text{(xvi)} \quad \frac{d \; r \; s \; r \; \text{əs} \; d}{P_s \, P_o \, P_a \text{ Caus. Root Asp.}}$$

ddsr'əsd "I made him/her hit them." Sentences of the forms xiv and xvi are derived, undoubtedly, by a generalized transformation that embeds the causative and its agent into the simple sentences of forms xiii and xv. In these sentences, no independent nominals, with which the concord elements may be said to be in agreement, have been expressed; this is not, of course, the usual state of affairs.

The potential morpheme may occur in causative sentences, and if so, the concord element in agreement with the agent P_a is attracted to a position immediately preceding it. Thus, a rule such as the following is required:

$$\text{(T.4)} \quad \frac{\text{Potential } X \, P_a}{1 \quad 2 \; 3} \quad \rightarrow 3 + 1 \quad 2 \quad \phi$$

Thus, in sentences containing both the potential and causative constituents, both rules T.3 and T.4 apply. With class 1 verb roots, the application of these two rules does not effect any change in the order of the concord elements. Thus, if we are given an underlying string,

(*a*) $P_o P_s P_a$ Caus. Root$_1$ Asp. Pot.

application of rule T.3 yields

(*b*) $P_o P_s$ Pot. P_a Caus. Root$_1$ Asp.

and then rule T.4 yields

(*c*) $P_o P_s P_a$ Pot. Caus. Root$_1$ Asp.

with the *P*'s in the same order as in example *a*. For example:

(xvii) $\begin{array}{ccccccccc} s & gy & y & l & z\vartheta & m & r & \int y\vartheta & d \\ P_o & \text{Neg.} & P_s & P_a & \text{Pot.} & \text{Neg.} & \text{Caus.} & \text{Root} & \text{Asp.} \end{array}$

sgyylz'əmrʃyd "she couldn't make him kill me." With class 2 verb roots, however, application of these two rules produces an order of the concord elements that is different from the underlying order; given the underlying string,

(*a'*) $P_s P_o P_a$ Caus. Root$_2$ Asp. Pot.

application of rule T.3 yields

(*b'*) P_s Pot. $P_o P_a$ Caus. Root$_2$ Asp.

and then rule T.4 yields

(*c'*) $P_s P_a$ Pot. P_o Caus. Root$_2$ Asp.

with the *P*'s in a different order in the derived string than is found in the underlying string. For example,

(xviii) $\begin{array}{ccccccccc} s & gy & y & z\vartheta & l & m & r & \vartheta s & d \\ P_s & \text{Neg.} & P_a & \text{Pot.} & P_o & \text{Neg.} & \text{Caus.} & \text{Root} & \text{Asp.} \end{array}$

sgyyzlmr'əsd "he couldn't make me hit her."

What Allen observed was that the sequence of concord elements in verbal complexes such as form xviii is not a true reflection of their grammatical order, where by order he meant the sequence in which the elements are found in example *a'*. Thus Allen associated the term *sequence* with what we may consider to be "derived constituent structure" — the structure displayed by sentences in their actual phonetic form — and *order* with "underlying constituent structure" — the structure displayed by sentences prior to the application of transformations. Thus, at this point, Allen supplied a fairly deep and significant interpretation for Firth's technical terms *sequence* and *order* (see earlier, p. 66):

> The peculiarities of exponential *sequence* associated with the Potential in three-pronoun complexes containing class 2 roots are thus not reflected in the *order* of grammatical structure. Concord relationships are relationships between elements of grammatical structure and not between phonetic data; and the concord-patterns of the Potential are thus the same as those of the non-potential. (pp. 158–159)

This is, of course, only an isolated instance of such an insight, and certainly does not mean in general that the difference between order and sequence in London school descriptions is taken to mean the difference between underlying and derived structure.

A few remarks are in order concerning the nature of the phrase structure component of the Abaza grammar. Of course, Allen has not described Abaza structure from the point of view of separating and distinguishing between the phrase structure and transformational component of the Abaza grammar; but on the basis of his description, a few things may be pretty fairly determined about the phrase structure. Unfortunately, since Allen chose to discuss only a very limited aspect of the structure of Abaza, even of the verb itself, it is not possible to give a particularly well motivated account of Abaza phrase structure on the basis of his description; knowledge of the structure of verbs in subordinate clauses and in interrogative sentences is obviously required. There seems to be sufficient evidence for believing that the verbal complex consists of two major constituents, which we may call the Verb and the Auxiliary, respectively. The Auxiliary comprises such constituents as Negative, Directional, Repetitive, Potential, Tense, and Aspect, while the Verb is made up of the concord elements, Preverb and Root. The following rules may be suggested as some sort of first approximation to the phrase structure rules of Abaza:

(P.1) $S \rightarrow NP\ VP$ Aux.

(P.2) $VP \rightarrow \ldots$ Verb   (where . . . indicates the other constituents dominated by VP, such as NP)

(P.3)   Aux. $\rightarrow$ (Neg.) (Dir.) (Repet.) (Pot.) (Tense) Asp.

(P.4)   Verb $\rightarrow P_s\,P_o\,P_i$ (Preverb) Root

The rule that classifies roots according to whether or not rule T.1 applies, may be stated as a lexical classification rule:

(C.1′)   Root → Root$_{\{1,2\}}$

Since there is a subclassification of the preverbs, according to the class of the root with which it occurs, we also need the lexical rule (p. 163):

(C.2)   Preverb → Preverb$_{\{1,2\}}$/ — Root$_{\{1,2\}}$

In the derived constituent structure, the various members of the auxiliary are scattered throughout the verbal complex; some, like the negative and the repetitive, are often or always discontinuous. We have already given the transformational rules that govern the position of the potential in the derived constituent structure. The concord elements, labeled P, occurring in the verb are "dummies" for which concord elements are substituted by agreement transformations. The motivation for considering them as being indicated in the phrase structure is that the agreement transformations must be put near or at the end of the transformational component, since the concord elements agree with the subject and object not of the underlying structure but of the derived structure. Rules that occur before these agreement transformations may have to refer to these concord elements, so it is useful to have them designated already in the phrase structure. We may adopt as a convention that if any P (such as P_i or P_o in the case of pure intransitive verbs) is not filled by any actual element, it is deleted.

4.6 J. Carnochan on Hausa (1951, 1952, 1957)

Carnochan's phonological study of Hausa was, according to his own testimony, deeply influenced by Firth right at the time of his publication of "Sounds and Prosodies":

> It was during the visit I made to the Northern Provinces of Nigeria in 1948, to study the phonetics and phonology of Hausa, that I became increasingly aware of a prosodic approach in linguistic research. My previous work under Professor J. R. Firth had already put me on the way towards using such an approach, but I had not advanced very far. Professor Firth read his paper on 'Sounds and prosodies' to this society shortly before my departure for Nigeria, and my research in the field, and my methods of stating the linguistic facts have been profoundly influenced by it. (1952, p. 78)

The published results of this study are contained in the three papers mentioned in footnote 5.

The contents of the first paper can be summarized as follows: there is a phonological distinction between long and short vowels in Hausa (not noted explicitly in the orthography), but the feature that distinguishes them is glottalization, since utterance-final short vowels are "closed" with the glottal stop. This single piece of evidence hardly constitutes justification for this feature identification, but there is no point in disputing the claim here. Carnochan went on to observe that the distinction between long and short vowels is neutralized in word-final position in nouns preceding the possessive pronoun enclitic. All such vowels are long before the enclitic *na* "my," and short before all the others, which are also all of the phonological structure *CCV*.

In the second paper, Carnochan again insisted that it is the glottalization feature that distinguishes long vowels from short ones, and he identified this feature with the one whose consonantal properties we have already discussed (on p. 68).

From the discussion in this paper, it can easily be determined that vowel length is neutralized when vowels occur before two consonants; thus we find *cika:*, *so:ka:*, *muska:*, but no **mu:ska:*, and so on. Surprisingly Carnochan gave no indication that he noticed this fact, although it can be determined directly from his notation for writing Hausa prosodically, as follows. Vowel length is indicated formulaically by a raised ^{v} following the vowel, thus *so^{v}ka*, and shortness by a raised $^?$, thus *ci$^?$ka*. But the signs ^{v} and $^?$ are considered representative of syllable-final prosodies, and hence are attached (along with the sign ^{h}) not to the vowel that is followed by two consonants but to the first of these consonants; thus *mus^{h}ka:*. When attached to consonants in these cases, ^{h} indicates voicelessness of the preceding consonant, ^{v} voicing, and $^?$ glottalization. Since vowels that appear before two consonants are not marked for length, it follows that if Carnochan's analysis is correct, vowels are not distinctively long when they precede two consonants. We see, in particular, that since inherent length may be neutralized before a suffix beginning with two consonants (for instance, all of the possessive pronouns except for the first person singular), there is a possibility that vowels may be distinctively long or short before two consonants throughout the language. If this is true, however, Carnochan's results published so far will not lead us to it.

Carnochan's third paper on Hausa is, if anything, of even more restricted significance than his preceding two. In it, he describes a certain class of "verbal nouns" as being derived from verbs by means of a suffix that duplicates and lengthens the final consonant of the verb stem. Thus from the stem *jef*, the verbal noun stem *jef+aff* is formed, to which may be added suffixes indicating number and gender. Before the masculine and feminine singular endings (orthographically *e* and *iya*), geminate *t, d, s, z* are palatalized to geminate *č, j, š,* and ǰ, respectively. Thus, from *fit*, the masculine and feminine singular verbal nouns *fitačče* and *fitaččiya* are formed; the plural common gender form is *fitattu*. The glottalized pre-palatals *ɗ* and *ts* are not affected by this palatalization rule, thus *daɗaɗɗe* derives from the stem *daɗ*. The remainder of the paper discusses gemination that arises under other circumstances in various Hausa dialects, but the facts themselves are very elementary.

While we shall not concern ourselves with the details here, it should be clear that Carnochan's prosodic notation can be easily converted into a long-component notation.

4.7 R. H. Robins on Sundanese (1957)

Robins' description of Sundanese vowel nasality was published in *Studies in Linguistic Analysis* to illustrate "within a delimited and relatively restricted field in a language, the use and application of prosodic abstractions in phonological statement" (1957, p. 87). The conditions under which nasalized vowels occur in Sundanese may be described very simply:

. . . once nasality has been initiated by the articulation of a nasal consonant, . . . it continues irrespective of syllable boundaries until checked. . . . Nasality is checked by:
1. A word boundary.
2. A supraglotally articulated consonant, i.e., any consonant other than *h* or *ʔ*. A second or subsequent nasal consonant in a word may be regarded as the check point of previously initiated nasality and as initiating subsequent nasality. (p. 90)

To describe these facts, Robins proposed the following notation:

In the case of words in which there are syllables with nasalized vowels whose nasality is to be regarded as initiated by a preceding nasal consonant, the extension of *n* the nasal prosody within the word may be symbolized phonologically by writing ‾‾‾‾‾ over the C and V elements of the syllables that are concerned. The C element to which this initiating consonant may be referred in the symbolization will be a focal point of *n* in the word. (pp. 91–92)

In this case, Robins' *n* prosody can be considered a long component with no alteration of the notation, and it is clear that the rule corresponding to his analysis is simply

(1) $[+\text{voc}] \rightarrow [+\text{nsl}]/[+\text{nsl}][-\text{cns}]_o$ —

There are words in Sundanese, however, for which rule 1 does not correctly predict vowel nasality. These words are all verbs in which the plural infix *ar/al* occurs immediately following a word-initial nasal consonant. For example, in the word *m+ar+iak*, not only is the vowel *a* of the infix nasalized, as one would expect from rule 1, but also the *a* of the verb stem, even though the consonant *r* intervenes between it and the preceding *m*. Furthermore, the *i* preceding this nasalized *a* is not nasalized. In general, "the third and following syllables of the -*ar*/*al*- infixed forms are also characterized by nasalization" (p. 93). This results in a phonetic contrast of nasalization between such forms as *m+ar+iak* [māriāk] and marios [mārios]. To account for the pronunciation of such forms as *m+ar+iak*, Robins devised a notation for expressing these facts, which corresponds to the following rule (an amendment of rule 1):

(1') [+voc] → [+nsl]/[+nsl](+Plural + [   ])[−cns]ₒ —

Rule 1' applies to a form like *m+ar+iak* as follows. First apply rule 1' in its full form. The only vowel that is in the environment [+nas] + Plural + [   ][−cns]ₒ — is the vowel *a* of the verb stem. Upon application of rule 1' in its full form, the resulting pronunciation is *m+ar+iāk*. Rule 1' in its short form, that is, the rule that results from disregarding the elements in parentheses, also applies to this form, since the *a* of the plural infix is in the environment [+nas][−cns]ₒ —, and hence is nasalized, yielding *m+ār+iāk*. In a similar way, the correct assignment of vowel nasality is given to all such forms with the plural infix.

We have already discussed Robins' contention (on pp. 58–59) that his prosodic analysis is superior to any possible phonemic analysis, indicating that in fact he failed to show that a phonemic analysis cannot be introduced without complicating the description. We see now that a phonemic analysis can be so introduced; we need merely consider the "long" form of rule 1' to be a morphophonemic rule, and its output to be a phonemic transcription; it is the phonemic transcription suggested by Stockwell in his review of *Studies in Linguistic Analysis* (1959, p. 258). The "short" form of rule 1 may be considered the usual sort of rule that expresses the distribution of allophones (in this case the nasalized allophones of each of the vowels in Sundanese).

4.8 T. F. Mitchell on Arabic (1960)

Mitchell's paper, which is an extensive discussion of accentuation and other phonological phenomena related to syllable structure in Classical Arabic and in several modern dialects, is one of the most brilliant exemplifications of prosodic analysis ever to have appeared.

Yet in it there is absolutely no mention of Firth, or of other members of the London school, and very little use is made of the terminology of that school.

The paper opens with a discussion of the accentuation of Classical Arabic words as they are taught in Cairo. According to Mitchell's account, the final syllable of a word is accented if it is a monosyllable, or if its final syllable is long; that is, if that syllable ends either in a long vowel followed by one or more consonants or in a short vowel followed by two consonants. Thus, *ḍarábt, ʕä ɛmääl, yätäḥäddäwn.*[11]

If the final syllable is not long, then it is not accented; thus disyllabic words with nonlong final syllables are accented on their first syllable: *ráʕaa, qáalat, ʃäädä, qúmtum.* For words having three or more syllables, the following rules hold. If the prefinal syllable is closed, that is, if it has the form *CVC*, *CVV*, or *CVVC*, then it is accented: *kätäbta, kitääbäh, mumääddä, hääδääni, muʃtaqqatääni, yätäqaatälúunä.* If, however, the prefinal syllable is open (having the form *CV*), then either that syllable is accented, or the syllable preceding it is, whichever one is an odd number of syllables following the last closed syllable in the word, or if there are none, whichever one is an odd number of syllables from the beginning of the word (counting the first syllable as being one syllable from the beginning of the word). Thus the following words are accented on the prefinal syllable: *käätäbä, qattälät, mäktäbäh, ḥääqqátun; ʕädwiyätúhu, mäɛrifätúhu, murtäbiṭátun, ʃäjarátun, kätäbätää; ʃäjaratuhúmää, baqaratuhúmää,* while the following are accented on the syllable preceding the prefinal syllable: *ʕinkäsara, ʕiḍtárabä, bulähníyätun, kätäbä, ʃäjarah; ʕädwiyätúhumää, mäɛrifätúhumää, ʃäjarátuhu, baqarátuhu.*

In generative phonological terms, these facts can be stated by means of a single rule having three parts, as follows:

$$
(1) \quad \begin{bmatrix} +\text{voc} \\ -\text{cns} \end{bmatrix} \rightarrow [+\text{acc}] \Big/ \begin{cases} (a) \begin{Bmatrix} \#\,C - C_o\,\# \\ -\,C_2\,\# \end{Bmatrix} \\ (b) \; -C_2 VC'\,\# \\ (c) \begin{Bmatrix} C_2 \\ \#\,C \end{Bmatrix}(VCVC)_o - (CV)CV(C)\,\# \end{cases}
$$

[11] For reading the transcribed Arabic forms, the following conventions may be used: θ, δ are voiceless and voiced dental fricatives; ʃ, j voiceless and voiced palatal fricatives (j is an affricate in Egyptian dialects); r alveolar flap; x, ɣ uvular fricatives; ḥ, ɛ pharyngeal fricatives; q uvular stop; ʕ glottal stop; ṭ, ḍ, ṣ emphatic consonants; i half-close front spread vowel, close when final or long; u half-close back to central vowel, rounded (Egypt), unrounded (Cyrenaica), close rounded when final or long (all dialects); ä, a front and back open vowels; e, o (Egypt only) mid- to half-close front and back vowels, spread and rounded, respectively. The acute accent indicates an accented vowel.

In rule 1, the symbol *C* is to be interpreted to mean any nonvowel or the second mora of a long vowel; the symbol *V* therefore stands just for a short vowel or the first mora of a long vowel.

Mitchell goes on to point out that the accentuation of Classical Arabic depends upon where it is taught. In Lebanon and Palestine, for example, the counterparts to words such as *käätăbä* and *fäjarátun* are pronounced *kăätăbä* and *fájáratun*, respectively, while in Upper Egypt, they are pronounced *kăätabä* and *fájaratun* (at least in connected discourse). In general, in Palestinian and Lebanese Classical Arabic, the accent of words not covered by parts *a* and *b* of rule 1 falls on the syllable preceding the prefinal syllable, while in Upper Egyptian Classical Arabic, it falls on the first syllable of the word.[12]

The accentuation of modern colloquial Egyptian Arabic is also almost completely accounted for by rule 1; the one major difference being that, in the modern colloquial, final long vowels are accented, for example, *gatóo* "cake," *mäskää* "holding (feminine singular) him." Mitchell specifically rejected the view of R. S. Harrell that stress must be considered phonemic, on the grounds of such minimal pairs as [síkit] "he was silent" and [sikít] "I was silent/you (masculine singular) were silent." If the second of these is represented as *sikítt* (which is justified on morphological grounds, since *-t* is the suffix indicating first person or second person masculine singular), then the accentuation of this form follows automatically from rule 1. Mitchell points out also that although the length of a double consonant at the end of a word is not significantly greater than that of a single consonant, it is articulated with greater tenseness. The length of the pretonic syllables is also affected. For other criticisms by Mitchell of Harrell's phonemic approach to colloquial Egyptian Arabic phonology, see Mitchell (1958).

In modern colloquial Cairo Arabic, moreover, unstressed noninitial high short vowels in open syllables are elided. Examples given by Mitchell include *fíhim* "he understood" but *fíhmit* (underlying *fihim+it*) "she understood"; *yääxud* "he takes" but *yáxdu* (underlying *yääxud+u*) "they take." Note also in this form that after application of the elision rule, a rule applies to shorten long vowels occurring before consonant clusters. Stressed short high vowels in open syllables are not elided, thus *yíktib* "he writes" but *yiktíbu* "they write"; nor are low vowels elided, thus *dárab* "he hit," *dárabit* "she hit." The rule also applies to delete word-initial unstressed high short vowels in open syllables when they occur in phrases following other words; thus

---

[12] In Lebanese Classical Arabic, word-final long vowels are accented if the long vowel is an indication of dual number; otherwise posttonic long vowels are shortened.

hudúumäk "your clothes," *ʕiddíini hdúumäk* "give me your clothes"; *ḥuséen* "Husein," *ʕäbu ḥséen* "Husein's father." On the other hand, we have also *faríid* "Fareed," *ʕäbu faríid* "Fareed's father"; *εúmar* "Omar," *ʕäbu εúmar* "Omar's father."

The rules required to account for these facts are the rules of stress assignment (rule 1 appropriately modified) together with the following rules:

$$(2) \quad \begin{bmatrix} +\text{voc} \\ -\text{cns} \\ +\text{dif} \\ -\text{acc} \end{bmatrix} \rightarrow \phi \Big/ [\ \ ]C - CV$$

$$(3) \quad \begin{bmatrix} +\text{voc} \\ -\text{cns} \end{bmatrix} \rightarrow \phi \Big/ \begin{bmatrix} +\text{voc} \\ -\text{cns} \end{bmatrix} - C_2$$

In addition, Mitchell points out that in trisyllabic words of the form *CiCiCä* or *CuCuCä*, the accent falls on the prefinal syllable, not upon the initial syllable as one would have expected. Thus one has in colloquial Cairo Arabic such forms as *ḍubúεä*, *ḥiṣínä*, *ɣiríbä*, but *búxälä*, *εínäbä*, and *kåtäbä*. The reason for this exceptional stress assignment, apparently, is to protect the prefinal high vowel from deletion according to rule 2.[13] If the initial syllable were stressed, we would obtain **ḍúbεä*, **ḥíṣnä*, and **ɣírbä*, since rule 2 would apply to delete the unstressed prefinal high vowel. Here we have an interesting case of an exceptional accentuation pattern developing so as to prevent the application of a later rule of vowel elision.

The remainder of Mitchell's paper is devoted to an account of the interrelation between accentuation, vowel elision, vowel insertion (anaptyxis), and vowel quality in a Bedouin dialect of the Cyrenaica Jebel in Libya. He noted that there are a large number of minimal pairs in this dialect distinguished by stress placement alone, for example, *íktib* "write!" versus *iktíb* "books." Because of such pairs, the phonemicist is obliged to consider stress placement as phonemic in this dialect. But to do so, Mitchell contended, would be at best unrevealing; a phonemic solution of this type would fail to account for a number of facts related to this apparent phonemic placement of stress; for example, when the suffix *-ih* is added to *íktib*, the resulting form is *íkitbih* "write it!" whereas when it is added to *iktíb* the result is *kítbih* "his books." It is the alternation of stress placement in related forms that demands phonological explanation.

---

[13] This point was not made by Mitchell.

The rule of accentuation in this dialect is different in a number of significant respects from that of colloquial Cairo Arabic; for one thing, dissyllables of the form *CVCVC* are stressed on the final syllable, thus *kitáb* "he wrote." In words of three or more underlying syllables, if both the prefinal and the syllable preceding the prefinal are open, the prefinal syllable is accented if it contains a low vowel; otherwise the initial syllable is accented. The reasons for formulating the rules of stress assignment in this way will become clear as soon as we have shown how the rules of elision of vowels in this dialect operate.

As in colloquial Cairo Arabic, an unstressed high vowel in an open syllable is elided in the Cyrenaica dialect. Thus we have *gássim* "divide up!" *gässímhä* "divide it (feminine) up!" but *gássmih* (underlying *gässimih*) "divide it (masculine) up!" Unlike Cairo Arabic, however, the rule also applies to such vowels in word-initial syllables; thus we have *kítbih* (underlying *kitibih*) "his books" but *iktib* (underlying *kitib*) "books" — the initial *i* in this form is an anaptyctic vowel. Moreover, an underlying low vowel in an open syllable is made into a high vowel. Thus, *gássäm* "he divided up," *gässámhä* "he divided it (feminine) up," but *gássimih* (underlying *gässämih*) "he divided it (masculine) up."

One other vowel elision rule is also required. To see this, first consider the form *kitáb* "he wrote." Since the vowel of the first syllable has not been elided, it must be an underlying low vowel; the underlying form of this word must therefore be *kätäb* (which also turns out to be the Classical Arabic phonetic form). Next, consider the word *iktíbät* "she has written." This word must be considered to have the underlying form *kätäbät*, where *-ät* is the third person feminine singular suffix in this particular conjugation. The stress assignment rule and the rule that raises low vowels in open syllables would incorrectly yield the form **kitíbät*. We cannot assume that the high vowel elision rule would apply to the first *i* of this form, since that rule must apply *before* the application of the rule that raises low vowels (otherwise all unstressed vowels in open syllables would be deleted). Therefore, we require a rule that deletes an unstressed low vowel in an open syllable when it precedes another open syllable. The phonological derivation of *iktíbät* from underlying *kätäbät* will then be as follows: *kätäbät* → (stress assignment) *kätábät* → (deletion of unstressed vowel in first of two open syllables) *ktábät* → (raising of low vowels in open syllables) *ktíbät* → (anaptyxis) *iktíbät*.

We may now formulate the rule of anaptyxis for the Cyrenaica dialect. This rule inserts a high vowel between the first and second nonvowels of a succession of three nonvowels, where initial and final word boundaries count as nonvowels. Thus any word that winds up with two initial consonants, upon application of the rules of vowel elision, will have an anaptyctic vowel inserted before the first of these consonants, whereas a word with two final consonants will have that vowel inserted between the two consonants, that is, in the environment $C_\alpha — C_\beta \#$. An example of the latter is provided by the word *kitåbit* "I wrote," which results from an underlying *kätäbt*. The rule is, however, inapplicable if the first two of the three consonants are identical; thus, from underlying *gässimih* "divide it (masculine) up!" we obtain *gåssmih* and not **gåsismih*; while from underlying *gäεmizu* "sit down!" we obtain *gåεimzu*.

Before proceeding, let us state formally the rules we have been informally discussing. The first is the rule that deletes an unstressed low vowel in an open syllable preceding another open syllable:

$$(4) \quad \begin{bmatrix} +\text{voc} \\ -\text{cns} \\ -\text{acc} \\ -\text{dif} \end{bmatrix} \rightarrow \phi \Big/ - CVCV$$

The next is the rule that deletes an unstressed high vowel in an open syllable (the Cyrenaica counterpart to rule 2):

$$(5) \quad \begin{bmatrix} +\text{voc} \\ -\text{cns} \\ -\text{acc} \\ +\text{dif} \end{bmatrix} \rightarrow \phi \Big/ - CV$$

Third is the rule that raises low vowels in open syllables:

$$(6) \quad \begin{bmatrix} +\text{voc} \\ -\text{cns} \\ -\text{dif} \end{bmatrix} \rightarrow [+\text{dif}] \Big/ - CV$$

Finally we have the rule of anaptyxis, which may be formulated as:

$$(7) \quad \phi \rightarrow \begin{bmatrix} +\text{voc} \\ -\text{cns} \\ +\text{dif} \\ -\text{grv} \end{bmatrix} \Big/ \begin{Bmatrix} \# \\ C_\alpha \end{Bmatrix} - \begin{Bmatrix} \# \\ C_\beta \end{Bmatrix} \quad \text{where } C_\alpha \neq C_\beta$$

The actual phonetic quality of a vowel in an open syllable depends upon its consonantal environment and also upon fairly complex rules of vowel harmony which affect stretches of two or sometimes more syllables. The "unmarked" quality of a vowel in an open syllable is *i*; if, however, it is in the neighborhood of an emphatic consonant it is [*u*], for example, *ṭuríig* "road," while in the neighborhood of a uvular or pharyngeal consonant it is [*ä*], as in *ḥäʃíiʃ* "grass." We forgo a description of the vowel harmony rules for the time being and indicate now how the rules we have already established account for somewhat more complex forms in the Cyrenaica dialect than we have thus far considered.

First, consider the word *íngitäl* "he was killed." This word must have the underlying form *ingätäl*, from which we obtain the phonetic form by application of rule 1 (accentuation appropriately modified for the Cyrenaica dialect) and rule 6 (raising of low vowels in open syllables). Consider now *inigtílät* "she was killed." The underlying form of this word must be set up as *ingätälät*. Stress is assigned to the prefinal syllable, since both the prefinal syllable and the syllable preceding it are short syllables, and the vowel of the prefinal syllable is low, yielding *ingätálät*. Then, by rule 4, we obtain *ingtálät;* by rule 6, *ingtílat*, and by rule 7, *inigtílät*. Next, consider *yíngitil* "he will be killed." This has the underlying form *yingätil*, from which the phonetic form is obtained by rules 1 and 6. On the other hand, *yingítlu* "they will be killed" has the underlying form *yingätilu*, from which the phonetic form is derived as follows. First, stress must be assigned to the syllable preceding the prefinal syllable, since, as we observed earlier, stress cannot fall on a prefinal short high vowel in an open syllable; thus, *yingátilu*. Now observe that rules 5 and 6 must be assumed to apply *simultaneously* to this form, for if rule 5 were to apply first, we would incorrectly obtain **yingátlu*. But rule 6 cannot precede rule 5 for reasons that we have already given. Therefore, their application must be simultaneous, yielding in this case *yingítlu*, to which no subsequent rules apply. Fortunately, the collapse of rules 5 and 6 into a single rule is not an *ad hoc* step at all, since, first, they operate in identical environments, and second, they describe phonetically similar processes, namely, vowel weakening. The weakening of a low vowel makes it, in many languages (for example Latin), into a high vowel, while the weakening of a high vowel is loss of that vowel (as in Slavic).

As a final illustration of the application of these rules to related forms, consider the words *ʃujár* "trees," *iʃjúrah* "a tree," *iʃjurúttä* "her tree," *ʃújurtih* "his tree," and *ʃujurtáyn* "two trees." The underlying form of *ʃujár* is *ʃäjar* (which is also the Classical Arabic form). By rule 1 we obtain *ʃäjár* → (rule 6) *ʃijár* → (back vowel harmony) *ʃujár*. The underlying form of *iʃjúrah* is *ʃäjarit*, where *-it* is the so-called feminine singulative suffix. In word-final position, the *t* of this suffix becomes *h*. The derivation is as follows: *ʃäjarit* → (rule 1) *ʃäjárit* → (rule 4) *ʃjárit* → (rule 6) *ʃjúrit* → (rule 7) *iʃjúrit* → (back vowel harmony) *iʃjúrut* → (*t* → *h* in the suffix *-it*) *iʃjúruh* → (lowering of back vowel before final guttural consonant) *iʃjúrah*.

Underlying *iʃjurúttä* we have *ʃäjarithä*, from which we obtain the phonetic form as follows: *ʃäjarithä* → (rule 1) *ʃäjaríthä* → (rule 4) *ʃjaríthä* → (rule 6) *ʃjuríthä* → (rule 7) *iʃjuríthä* → (back vowel harmony) *iʃjurúthä*. Finally, when a suffix beginning with *h* follows a voiceless consonant, the consonant is geminated and the *h* is lost; thus, *iʃjurúthä* → *iʃjurúttä*. Underlying *ʃújurtih* we have *ʃäjaritih*, a form that has three initial open syllables. Since the prefinal vowel is not a low vowel, stress is assigned to the initial syllable, yielding *ʃä́jaritih*. If we apply rules 4, 5, and 7 to this form, however, we obtain, incorrectly, **ʃä́jurtih*. In order to obtain the observed phonetic form, we must assume that rules 4, 5, and 6 are all applied simultaneously and not just rules 5 and 6. Rule 6 applies to the vowel of the initial syllable, raising it to *i*; rule 4 applies to the vowel of the second syllable, deleting it; and rule 5 applies to the third syllable, deleting it also, yielding *ʃíjrtih* → (rule 7) *ʃíjurtih* → (harmony of back vowels) *ʃújurtih*. The word *ʃujurtä̊yn*, which has as its underlying form *ʃäjaritayn*, presents another problem, since stress is assigned to the final syllable; the first syllable therefore being subject to deletion by rule 4. To prevent it from being deleted, we must restrict the environment of application of rule 4 to unstressed low vowels in open syllables that precede exactly one open syllable. If we do so, then the derivation of *ʃujurtä̊yn* proceeds in exactly the same way as that of *ʃújurtih*.

The rule of harmony works essentially as follows: The unmarked short vowel *i* (either in an open or closed syllable) becomes *u* in a syllable preceding or following an open syllable containing a short back vowel (either *u* or *a*); and a short vowel in a syllable following an open syllable containing a low vowel (either *ä* or *a*) becomes low. We have given a number of examples illustrating back vowel harmony. The following examples illustrate low vowel harmony. From underlying *θäɛälib* "fox," we obtain the phonetic form *iθɛä̊läb* as follows: *θäɛälib* → (rule 1) *θäɛálib* → (rule 4) *θɛä̊lib* → (rule 6) *θɛílib* → (rule 7) *iθɛílib* (lowering of short vowels in open syllables in neighborhood of guttural consonants) *iθɛälib* → (low vowel harmony) *iθɛä̊läb*. In the case of *umɛáraf* "claws," both back harmony and low harmony have taken place. The underlying form is *maɛaruf*, from which we obtain the phonetic form as follows: *maɛaruf* → (rule 1) *maɛáruf* → (rule 4) *mɛáruf* → (rule 6) *mɛúruf* → (rule 7) *imɛúruf* → (lowering of short vowels in neighborhood of guttural consonants) *imɛáruf* → (back vowel harmony) *umɛáruf* → (low vowel harmony) *umɛáraf*.

4.9 J. T. Bendor-Samuel on Terena (1960, 1962)

The first of J. T. Bendor-Samuel's recently published studies of the Terena language, of the Arawakan family, spoken in Mato Grosso, Brazil, deals with the first and second person singular pronouns. Generally, these morphemes do not have any phonological segments associated with them, but when they are present they have an effect on other segments, which Bendor-Samuel called prosodic. The facts are briefly as follows. When the first person singular pronoun is attached to a noun or verb, all the vowels and glides are nasalized in that word, up to the first obstruent, starting at the beginning of the word. This obstruent, if there is any, is then voiced, and a homorganic nasal segment precedes it. The voiced counterparts to the voiceless fricatives that Bendor-Samuel writes *h* and *hy* are both *ž* (which is also the voiced counterpart to *š*). Thus: *'ayo* "his brother," *'ãỹõ* "my brother"; *e'moʔu* "his word," *ẽ'mõʔũ* "my word"; *'owoku* "his house," *'õw̃õŋgu* "my house"; *a'hyaʔašo* "he desires," *ã'nžaʔaso* "I desire," and so on. When a second person singular pronoun is attached to a noun or verb, if the following word begins with a vowel, a *y*-glide is prefixed to the word. Thus: *o'topiko* "he cut down," *yo'topiko* "you cut down." If the word begins with a consonant, then the first non-*i* vowel undergoes a change. If it is *a* or *o*, it becomes *e*; if *e* or *u*, it becomes *i*. Thus *ku'rikena* "his peanut," *ki'rikena* "your peanut"; *'piho* "he went," *'pihe* "you went." If all of the vowels of the word are identically *e*, then they are all raised to *i*: *'nene* "his tongue," *'nini* "your tongue," and so on. In certain bisyllabic nouns, the underlying vowel is not completely replaced by the new vowel, but is retained after the new vowel: *'tuti* "his head," *'tiuti* "your head"; *'paho* "his mouth," *'peaho* "your mouth." It may be possible to account for these last examples by representing the first vowel as a double vowel: *'tuuti* and *'paaho;* if this can be done, and Bendor-Samuel has given no reason for excluding the possibility, then these forms would also be regular.

Bendor-Samuel considered the first person singular form to be represented by a nasalization prosody whose focus is the beginning of the word to which it is attached, and whose domain is the sequence of segments up to the first obstruent, or the end of the word if there are no obstruents in the word. This is to say, in effect, that there are the following phonological rules in the language:

(1) $I + Sg. \rightarrow [+\text{nsl}]$

(2) $[-\text{cns}] \rightarrow [+\text{nsl}]/ \# [+\text{nsl}] + [-\text{obs}]_o —$

(3) $\begin{bmatrix} +\text{voc} \\ +\text{nsl} \\ 1 \end{bmatrix} \begin{matrix} [+\text{obs}] \\ \\ 2 \end{matrix} \rightarrow 1 \begin{bmatrix} 2 \\ +\text{nsl} \end{bmatrix} + \begin{bmatrix} 2 \\ +\text{voi} \end{bmatrix}$

(4) $[+\text{nsl}] \rightarrow \phi/ \# — +$

Special rules will also be required to collapse the voiced counterparts of *š*, *h*, and *hy* into *ž*. Similarly, Bendor-Samuel defined the second person singular form to be represented by a palatalizing prosody, whose behavior is given by the rules:

(5) $II + Sg. \rightarrow \begin{bmatrix} -\text{cns} \\ -\text{voc} \\ -\text{grv} \end{bmatrix}$

(6) $\begin{Bmatrix} \begin{Bmatrix} [+\text{dff}] \\ [-\text{grv}] \end{Bmatrix} \\ {}_1 [+\text{grv}] \end{Bmatrix}_1 \rightarrow \begin{Bmatrix} \begin{bmatrix} +\text{dff} \\ -\text{grv} \end{bmatrix} \\ {}_1 \begin{bmatrix} -\text{grv} \\ -\text{cmp} \end{bmatrix} \end{Bmatrix}_1$

$\Big/ \# \begin{bmatrix} -\text{cns} \\ -\text{voc} \\ -\text{grv} \end{bmatrix} + C \Big(\begin{bmatrix} +\text{voc} \\ -\text{grv} \end{bmatrix} C\Big)_o \overline{[+\text{voc}]}$

(7) $\begin{bmatrix} -\text{cns} \\ -\text{voc} \\ -\text{grv} \end{bmatrix} \rightarrow \phi \Big/ \# - + C$

As formulated, these rules do not give the correct form for *II+Sg.+nene* "your tongue," and so on, but the rule can be modified appropriately to account for these forms as well.

A phonetic ambiguity can arise in Terena through application of rule 6. The form *'yeno* is the pronunciation of both *'yeno* "his wife" and *II+Sg.+yono* "you walked." This ambiguity causes no problems for the phonemicist, however, since it can be handled in a straightforward manner on the morphophonemic level; that is, the forms are morphophonemically distinct but phonemically identical, in the same way that the English homophone *lives* may be considered to represent two morphophonemically distinct entities, *layF* + *Plural* and *layv* + *Plural* (the latter meaning "opposite of 'stills.' ").

Bendor-Samuel's second paper on Terena deals with a much more significant topic than his first, namely, an account of the very intricate stress pattern of the language. He observed first that all words except certain particles can be stressed only on one or another of their first two syllables. This he called "primary placement stress." In certain grammatically defined contexts, however, nouns and verbs may be stressed on a later syllable, either the second or the third, and this he called "secondary placement stress." Nominal and verbal roots may be classified exhaustively according to which syllable is stressed. For example, words in which the verbal root *pih* "go home" occurs take primary placement stress on the second syllable and secondary placement stress on the third. This characteristic of the root *pih* must obviously be considered an abstractly represented feature of the root itself.

Over and above the rules that assign stress to words depending on the classification of their head root, there is a rule that prohibits stress from appearing on the final syllable of any word. Thus, where we would expect the forms **pi'ho*, under primary placement, and **piho'po*, under secondary placement stress, neither form occurs. Instead, the penult is stressed, but with different concomitants of pitch and length of the vowel and following consonant (from, say, *pi'hopo* under primary placement stress). Bendor-Samuel symbolized this stress quality with a grave accent; for typographical ease, we shall indicate it with the symbol *"*. Thus, in particular, for the starred forms, we find instead *"piho* and *pi"hopo*. This phenomenon we can express by a rule that will apply after the stress placement rules:

(8) $C_oV'C_oV \# \rightarrow \text{"}C_oVC_oV \#$

Bendor-Samuel then raised a question: If *piho* under primary placement stress is pronounced *"piho*, what is its stress under secondary placement stress? According to the classification of the root *pih*, it should be stressed on the third syllable, but obviously there is no third syllable in this word. The form that actually occurs is *'piho*. Suppose we try to derive this form from the stress assignment rules and rule 8. One way would be to say that if there is no syllable for the stress placement rule to assign stress to, then the stress is assigned to the last syllable of the word, and is moved by rule 8 back to the penult. But this will not work, because we would get *"piho* as before. Suppose that instead of ordinary stress, the stress we have symbolized by *"* is somehow assigned to the last syllable, and is moved back to the penult by a rule opposite in effect to rule 8:

(9) $C_oV''C_oV \# \rightarrow 'C_oVC_oV \#$

Clearly we can combine rules 8 and 9 into one rule that moves stress back one syllable from the end of the word and simply reverses the tonal gravity of the stress from what it was on the ultima. Making this tone, now, a property of the vowel, such a rule, carefully formulated, would read:

$$(8') \left\{ \begin{array}{l} (a) \begin{bmatrix} +\text{voc} \\ -\text{cns} \end{bmatrix} \rightarrow \begin{bmatrix} +\text{acc} \\ -\alpha\,\text{ton} \end{bmatrix} \Big/ - C_o \begin{bmatrix} +\text{acc} \\ \alpha\,\text{ton} \end{bmatrix} \# \\[12pt] (b) \begin{bmatrix} +\text{voc} \\ -\text{cns} \end{bmatrix} \rightarrow \begin{bmatrix} -\text{acc} \\ -\text{ton} \end{bmatrix} \Big/ - \# \end{array} \right\}$$

In rule 8′ the feature of tonality expresses the gravity of the pitch associated with the two kinds of stresses. It remains now to justify a rule that would assign grave tone and stress to the last syllable of *piho* under secondary stress assignment.

To do this, we need to understand the relationship between the occurrence of verbal and nominal forms with secondary placement stress and the grammatical contexts in which they occur. Bendor-Samuel presented what he claimed to be an exhaustive list of such contexts (1962, pp. 117–118), and in all of these contexts except two we find the verbal or nominal word standing in close syntactic parataxis with either a preceding or following particle. In those two cases, it does not seem unreasonable to suppose that some covert particle is present that is also in close parataxis with the verb. Now, let us assume that in all of these cases the verbal or nominal word together with these particles represent an immediate constituent in Terena sentences, which we may call noun or verb "extension," and let us suppose that there are no other instances of this constituent in sentences of different types from the ones listed by Bendor-Samuel. Given these assumptions, it is possible to account with a transformational cycle[14] for the occurrence of secondary placement stress by derivation from forms in which primary placement stress is made in the underlying form. In the first cycle, primary placement stress is made on all nouns and verbs in the language, and in the second cycle, which occurs only with the constituent "verb extension" or "noun extension," the stress is moved to a

[14] On the notion of a transformational cycle see, for example, N. Chomsky and G. A. Miller (1963, pp. 314 ff.).

secondary placement position. We can express (in words) the rules of the cycle as follows:

C.1. Secondary stress placement. The rule moves stress already assigned (*a*) onto the second or third syllable, depending upon the stress class of the main noun or verb root, or (*b*) to the last syllable of the word, if there is no syllable to bear the stress under (*a*).

C.2. Primary stress placement. The rule assigns stress and non-grave tone to the first or second syllable of the word, according to the stress class of the main root.

C.3. Rule 8′.

To demonstrate the applicability of these rules, we show how to derive the stress placement in the forms (i) *pi′kohiko* "they were afraid," (ii) *ina′maʔašo piko′hiko* "all the more they were afraid," (iii) *pi′hopo* "he went home," (iv) *inamaʔašo pi″hopo* "all the more he went home," (v) *″piho* "he went," (vi) *ina′maʔašo ′piho* "all the more he went," (vii) *″uto* "plate," (viii) *u′tohiko* "plates."

	Form	*Rule*
(i)	[pikohiko]$_V$	
	pi′kohiko	C.2 (*pik* takes primary placement stress on the second syllable)
(ii)	[[inamaʔašo]$_P$ [pikohiko]$_V$]$_{Ext.}$	
	[ina′maʔašo]$_P$ [pi′kohiko]$_V$	C.2
	[ina′maʔašo piko′hiko]$_{Ext.}$	new cycle; C.1
(iii)	[pihopo]$_V$	
	pi′hopo	C:2
(iv)	[[inamaʔašo]$_P$ [pihopo]$_V$]$_{Ext.}$	
	[ina′maʔašo]$_P$ [pi′hopo]$_V$	C.2
	[ina′maʔašo piho′po]$_{Ext.}$	n.c.; C.1
	[ina′maʔašo pi″hopo]$_{Ext.}$	C.3
(v)	[piho]$_V$	
	pi′ho	C.2
	″piho	C.3
(vi)	[[inamaʔašo]$_P$ [piho]$_V$]$_{Ext.}$	
	[ina′maʔašo]$_P$ [pi′ho]$_V$	C.2
	[ina′maʔašo]$_P$ [″piho]$_V$	C.3
	[ina′maʔašo pi″ho]$_{Ext.}$	n.c.; C.1
	[ina′maʔašo ′piho]$_{Ext.}$	C.3
(vii)	[uto]$_N$	
	u′to	C.2
	″uto	C.3
(viii)	[utohiko]$_N$	
	u′tohiko	C.2

Bendor-Samuel observed that the rules of stress placement in Terena are such that potential ambiguity between primary and secondary placement stress is always avoided. Oppositely placed stress either occurs on different syllables with the same tonality or on the same syllable with different tonality. Bendor-Samuel, in fact, expressed belief that the stress pattern of the language arose from an unconscious effort to prevent potential ambiguities. There is a certain attractiveness to this argument, but why, one may ask, is the real ambiguity of the form *'yeno* not similarly resolved? The interesting observation, I think, is that rules C.1 through C.3 organized in a transformational cycle are the simplest possible rules that prevent stress placement from assigning stress to the last syllable of words and that preserve distinctiveness by means of a tonal feature. In other words, if it turns out that the analysis just given of Terena stress is essentially correct, then we can say that the Terena child who hears such forms as *pi'kohiko, ina'maʔašo piko'hiko, ''piho, ina'maʔašo 'piho*, and who knows *a priori* that he is able to organize certain phonological rules into a transformational cycle, will necessarily choose this set of rules as part of his grammar for the language.

It will be noted that Bendor-Samuel did not attempt a "prosodic analysis" of the Terena stress pattern, and it is perhaps no accident that the three "deepest" phonological descriptions considered here, Allen's analysis of the Abaza verb, Mitchell's analysis of the vowel system of a Bedouin dialect, and Bendor-Samuel's study of Terena stress are not oriented prosodically but go well beyond the constraints imposed by the prosodic framework, as it has been developed by the London school.

4.10 F. R. Palmer, N. Waterson, and J. Carnochan on Vowel Harmony in Tigre, Turkish, and Igbo

The phenomenon of vowel harmony has been the object of analysis in a number of recent papers by members of the London school, and three have been singled out for consideration here. In the first of these, F. R. Palmer discussed the degree of openness in the nonclose (non-diffuse) short vowels of Tigre. He observed that an open-front variety [a] is found (i) when the nonclose short vowel is followed within a word by a long open-front vowel [a:] and no other long vowel intervenes, and (ii) when a pharyngeal or glottalized consonant follows in the same word, or if it is immediately preceded by such a consonant. Otherwise its quality is half open and central [ɒ]. This vowel is moreover slightly fronted when it precedes a front vowel, and slightly backed when it precedes a back (rounded) vowel. The notation Palmer devised to transcribe these facts is patently a long-component notation. Inspection of a few of his forms will readily confirm this observation. Thus, for [manka:hu] he writes $\alpha(CaCCV)w(CV)$; for [tʊko:bata:] he writes $w(CaCV)\alpha(CaCV)$, and so on. The features involved in these long components are moreover subphonemic.

Natalie Waterson's account of Turkish vowel harmony is of interest because of John Lyons' later interpretation of it as an analysis that is superior to any possible phonemic or morphophonemic analysis of Turkish (1962). Lyons proposed extracting two "word-prosodies" in Turkish, frontness/backness and rounded/nonrounded, leaving "openness" as the only exponent of phonematic vowels. Thus, he proposed analyzing the Turkish word that is phonemically /gözler/ as *FRgazlar*, /kïzlar/ as *BNkizler*, and so on, where the capital letters represent the word prosodies. But, obviously, this is long-component notation. Lyons apparently felt that it was a superior notation to all possible morphophonemic ones because it happens to be superior to the one morphophonemic notation that he compared it to (p. 131).[15]

Carnochan's analysis of Igbo vowel harmony in prosodic terms is also a long-componential analysis; no alterations in his notation have to be made to reveal this. Certain prosodies (or components) have as their domain a form of the verb and also their pronominal subject, such as the prosody of tongue height R/L, while others, such as gravity, have as their domain simply the verb. What Carnochan's analysis fails to reveal is that the indication of tongue-height class must be marked on the verb. The height of the vowel in the pronoun is clearly assimilated to the height class of the verb.

It may be pointed out that practically the same kind of vowel harmony (involving the same features and the same classes of vowels), plus an additional pair, one front and one back, is found in Twi; and for this language, Jack Berry has given an analysis of the harmony that satisfactorily reveals which vowel is assimilating which feature (1957).

[15] The morphophonemic analysis with which he compared it was that of C. F. Voegelin and M. E. Ellinghausen (1943).

Selected Bibliography

In this bibliography, the following abbreviations are used for the names of journals:

BSO(A)S: Bulletin of the School of Oriental (and African) Studies.
IJAL: International Journal of American Linguistics.
JAOS: Journal of the American Oriental Society.
TPS: Transactions of the Philological Society.

Allen, W. S., 1951. "Some Prosodic Aspects of Retroflexion and Aspiration in Sanskrit," *BSOAS, 13,* 939–946.
———, 1954. "Retroflexion in Sanskrit: Prosodic Technique and Its Relevance to Comparative Statement," *BSOAS, 16,* 556–565.
———, 1956. "Structure and System in the Abaza Verbal Complex," *TPS,* pp. 127–176.
———, 1957. "Aspiration in the Hāṛautī Nominal," in *Studies in Linguistic Analysis,* pp. 68–86.
Arnaud, A., 1662. *Port-Royal Logic* (trans. T. S. Baynes), Edinburgh, Scotland: W. Blackwell, 1850.
Bar-Hillel, Y., 1954. "Logical Syntax and Semantics," *Language, 30,* 230–237.
Bendor-Samuel, J. T., 1960. "Some Problems of Segmentation in the Phonological Analysis of Terena," *Word, 16,* 348–355.
———, 1962. "Stress in Terena," *TPS,* pp. 105–123.
Berry, J., 1957. "Vowel Harmony in Twi," *BSOAS, 19,* 124–130.
Bloomfield, L., 1933. *Language,* New York: Holt, Rinehart & Winston.
Bursill-Hall, G. L., 1961. " 'Levels' Analysis: J. R. Firth's Theories of Linguistic Analysis (Part II)," *Journal of the Canadian Linguistic Association, 6,* No. 3, 164–191.
Carnochan, J., 1951. "A Study of Quantity in Hausa," *BSOAS, 13,* 1032–1044.
———, 1952. "Glottalization in Hausa," *TPS,* pp. 78–109.

116

——, 1957. "Gemination in Hausa," in *Studies in Linguistic Analysis*, pp. 149–181.

——, 1960. "Vowel Harmony in Igbo," *African Language Studies, 1*, 155–163.

Chomsky, N., 1959. "Review of B. F. Skinner, *Verbal Behavior*," *Language, 35*, 26–58.

——, 1961. "Some Methodological Remarks on Generative Grammar," *Word, 17*, 219–239.

——, 1964. "Current Issues in Linguistic Theory," in Fodor and Katz, 1964, pp. 50–118.

——, 1965. *Aspects of the Theory of Syntax*, Cambridge, Mass.: The M.I.T. Press.

Chomsky, N., and G. A. Miller, 1963. "Introduction to the Formal Analysis of Natural Languages," in Luce, Bush, and Galanter, 1963, pp. 269–321.

Descartes, R., 1647. "Notes Directed Against a Certain Programme," in E. S. Haldane and G. R. T. Ross (editors), *The Philosophical Works of Descartes*, Vol. I, New York: Dover, 1955, pp. 429–450.

Dixon, R. M. W., 1963. *Linguistic Science and Logic*, The Hague, Netherlands: Mouton.

Firth, J. R., 1930, *Speech*, reprinted in Firth, 1964, pp. 139–211.

——, 1934a. "The Word 'Phoneme,' " reprinted in Firth, 1957c, pp. 1–2.

——, 1934b. "The Principles of Phonetic Notation in Descriptive Grammar," reprinted in Firth, 1957c, pp. 3–6.

——, 1935a. "The Technique of Semantics," reprinted in Firth, 1957c, pp. 7–33.

——, 1935b. "The Use and Distribution of Certain English Sounds," reprinted in Firth, 1957c, pp. 34–46.

——, 1935c. "Phonological Features of Some Indian Languages," reprinted in Firth, 1957c, pp. 47–53.

——, 1936. "Alphabets and Phonology in India and Burma," reprinted in Firth, 1957c, pp. 54–75.

——, 1937. *The Tongues of Men*, reprinted in Firth, 1964, pp. 1–138.

——, 1946. "The English School of Phonetics," reprinted in Firth, 1957c, pp. 92–120.

——, 1948a. "Sounds and Prosodies," reprinted in Firth, 1957c, pp. 121–138.

——, 1948b. "The Semantics of Linguistic Science," reprinted in Firth, 1957c, pp. 139–147.

——, 1949. "Atlantic Linguistics," reprinted in Firth, 1957c, pp. 156–172.

——, 1950. "Personality and Language in Society," reprinted in Firth, 1957c, pp. 177–189.

——, 1951a. "Modes of Meaning," reprinted in Firth, 1957c, pp. 190–215.

——, 1951b. "General Linguistics and Descriptive Grammar," reprinted in Firth, 1957c, pp. 216–228.

——, 1956. "Philology in the Philological Society," *TPS*, pp. 1–25.

——, 1957a. "A Synopsis of Linguistic Theory, 1930–1955," in *Studies in Linguistic Analysis*, pp. 1–32.

——, 1957b. "Ethnographic Analysis and Language with Reference to Malinowski's Views," in R. Firth, 1957, pp. 93–117.

———, 1957c. *Papers in Linguistics, 1934–1951*, London, England: Oxford University Press.

———, 1964. *The Tongues of Men and Speech*, London, England: Oxford University Press.

Firth, J. R., and H. J. F. Adam, 1950. "Improved Techniques in Palatography and Kymography," reprinted in Firth, 1957c, pp. 173–176.

Firth, J. R., and B. B. Rogers, 1937. "The Structure of the Chinese Monosyllable in a Hunanese Dialect (Changsha)," reprinted in Firth, 1957c, pp. 76–91.

Firth, R. (editor), 1957. *Man and Culture: An Evaluation of the Work of Bronislav Malinowski*, London, England: Routledge and Kegan Paul.

Fodor, J., and J. J. Katz (editors), 1964. *The Structure of Language: Readings in the Philosophy of Language.* Englewood Cliffs, N. J.: Prentice-Hall.

Gardiner, A. H., 1932. *The Theory of Speech and Language* (2nd ed. 1951), Oxford, England: Oxford University Press.

Haas, W., 1954. "On Defining Linguistic Units," *TPS*, pp. 54–84.

Halle, M., 1959. *The Sound Pattern of Russian*, The Hague, Netherlands: Mouton.

Halliday, M. A. K., 1957. "Some Aspects of Systematic Description and Comparison in Grammatical Analysis," in *Studies in Linguistic Analysis*, pp. 54–67.

———, 1959. *The Language of the Chinese "Secret History of the Mongols,"* Publication 17 of the Philological Society, Oxford, England: Basil Blackwell.

———, 1961. "Categories of a Theory of Grammar," *Word, 17*, 241–292.

Harris, Z. S., 1944. "Simultaneous Components in Phonology," reprinted in Joos, 1957, pp. 124–138.

———, 1951. *Structural Linguistics*, Chicago, Ill.: Chicago University Press.

Haugen, E., 1958. "Review of J. R. Firth, *Papers in Linguistics, 1934–1951,*" *Language, 34*, 498–502.

Henderson, E. J. A., 1949. "Prosodies in Siamese: A Study in Synthesis," *Asia Major* (n.s.), *1*, 189–215.

Hill, A. A., 1961. "Suprasegmentals, Prosodies, Prosodemes," *Language, 37*, 457–468.

Jakobson, R., and M. Halle, 1956. *Fundamentals of Language*, The Hague, Netherlands: Mouton.

Jones, D., 1950. *The Phoneme: Its Nature and Use*, Cambridge, England: Heffer.

Joos, M. (editor), 1957. *Readings in Linguistics*, Washington, D. C.: American Council of Learned Societies.

Katz, J., and J. Fodor, 1963. "The Structure of a Semantic Theory," *Language, 39*, 170–210.

Langendoen, D. T., 1964. "Review of *Studies in Linguistic Analysis*," *Language, 40*, 305–321.

———, forthcoming *a*. "Review of R. M. W. Dixon, *What Is Language?*" *Language*.

———, forthcoming *b*. "Review of C. E. Bazell, J. C. Catford, M. A. K. Halliday, and R. H. Robins (editors), *In Memory of J. R. Firth,*" *Foundations of Language*.

Leach, E. R., 1957. "The Epistemological Background to Malinowski's Empiricism," in R. Firth, 1957, pp. 119–138.

Luce, R. D., R. R. Bush, and E. Galanter (editors), 1963. *Handbook of Mathematical Psychology*, Vol. II, New York: Wiley.

Lyons, J., 1962. "Phonemic and Non-phonemic Phonology: Some Typological Reflections," *IJAL*, *28*, 127–134.

————, 1963. *Structural Semantics: An Analysis of Part of the Vocabulary of Plato*, Publication 20 of the Philological Society, Oxford, England: Basil Blackwell.

MacDonnell, A. A., 1916. *A Vedic Grammar for Students*, Oxford, England: Oxford University Press.

Malinowski, B., 1916. "Baloma: Spirits of the Dead in the Trobriand Islands," in Redfield, 1948, pp. 125–227.

————, 1920. "Classificatory Particles in the Language of Kiriwina," *BSOS*, *1*, Part 4, pp. 33–78.

————, 1922. *Argonauts of the Western Pacific*, London, England: G. Routledge.

————, 1923. "The Problem of Meaning in Primitive Languages," supplement to Ogden and Richards (10th ed. 1966), pp. 296–336.

————, 1926. *Crime and Custom in Savage Society*, Paterson, N. J.: Littlefield, Adams, 1959.

————, 1935. *Coral Gardens and Their Magic*, Vol. II, New York: American Book Company. Also reprinted 1965, Bloomington, Ind.: Indiana University Press.

Matthews, P. H., 1966. "The Concept of Rank in 'Neo-Firthian' Grammar," *Journal of Linguistics*, *2*, 101–110.

Mitchell, T. F., 1957. "The Language of Buying and Selling in Cyrenaica: A Situational Statement," *Hespéris*, *44*, 31–71.

————, 1958. "Review of R. S. Harrell, *The Phonology of Colloquial Egyptian Arabic*," *BSOAS*, *21*, 635–637.

————, 1960. "Prominence and Syllabification in Arabic," *BSOAS*, *23*, 369–389.

Mohrmann, C., F. Norman, and A. Sommerfelt, 1963. *Trends in Modern Linguistics*, Utrecht, Netherlands: Spectrum Press.

Ogden, C. K., and I. A. Richards, 1923. *The Meaning of Meaning* (10th ed. 1966), New York: Harcourt.

Palmer, F. R., 1956. " 'Openness' in Tigre: A Problem in Prosodic Statement," *BSOAS*, *18*, 561–577.

————, 1957. "Gemination in Tigrinya," in *Studies in Linguistic Analysis*, pp. 134–148.

————, 1958*a*. "Linguistic Hierarchy," *Lingua*, *7*, 225–241.

————, 1958*b*. "Comparative Statement and Ethiopian Semitic," *TPS*, pp. 119–143.

————, 1962. *The Morphology of the Tigre Noun*, London, England: Oxford University Press.

Pike, K. L., 1947. "Grammatical Prerequisites to Phonemic Analysis," *Word*, *3*, 155–172.

Postal, P., 1964. *Constituent Structure: A Study of Contemporary Models of Syntactic Description*, The Hague, Netherlands: Mouton.

————, 1966. "Review of Dixon, *Linguistic Science and Logic*," *Language*, 42, 84–93.

Redfield, R. (editor), 1948. *Magic, Science, and Religion and Other Essays*, Boston, Mass.: Beacon Press.

Robins, R. H., 1952. "Noun and Verb in Universal Grammar," *Language*, 28, 289–298.

————, 1953. "Formal Divisions in Sundanese," *TPS*, pp. 109–142.

————, 1957. "Vowel Nasality in Sundanese: A Phonological and Grammatical Study," in *Studies in Linguistic Analysis*, pp. 87–103.

————, 1959. "Nominal and Verbal Derivation in Sundanese," *Lingua*, 8, 337–369.

————, 1961. "John Rupert Firth," *Language*, 37, 191–200.

————, 1963. "General Linguistics in Great Britain 1930–1960," in Mohrmann, Norman, and Sommerfelt, 1963, pp. 11–37.

Sapir, E., 1925. "Sound Patterns in Language" reprinted in Joos, 1957, pp. 19–25.

Saussure, F. de, 1916. *Cours de linguistique générale* (5th ed. 1960), Paris, France: Payot.

Sharp, A. E., 1954. "A Tonal Analysis of the Disyllabic Noun in the Machame Dialect of Chaga," *BSOAS*, 16, 157–169.

Sprigg, R. K., 1957. "Junction in Spoken Burmese," in *Studies in Linguistic Analysis*, pp. 104–138.

————, 1961. "Vowel Harmony in Lhasa Tibetan: Prosodic Analysis Applied to Interrelated Vocalic Features of Successive Syllables," *BSOAS*, 24, 116–138.

Stockwell, R. P., 1959. "Review of *Studies in Linguistic Analysis*," *IJAL*, 29, 254–259.

Studies in Linguistic Analysis, 1957. Special publication of the Philological Society, Oxford, England: Basil Blackwell.

Twaddell, W. F., 1935. *On Defining the Phoneme*, reprinted in part in Joos, 1957, pp. 55–79.

Voegelin, C. F., and M. E. Ellinghausen, 1943. "Turkish Structure," *JAOS*, 63, 34–65.

Waterson, N., 1956. "Some Aspects of the Phonology of the Nominal Forms of the Turkish Word," *BSOAS*, 18, 578–591.

Wittgenstein, L., 1953. *Philosophical Investigations* (trans. G. E. M. Anscombe), New York: MacMillan.

Index